CAPTURING CUSTOMERS' HEARTS

FINANCIAL TIMES

Prentice Hall

In an increasingly competitive world, it is quality
of thinking that gives an edge – an idea that opens new
doors, a technique that solves a problem, or an insight
that simply helps make sense of it all.

We work with leading authors in the fields of
management and finance to bring cutting-edge thinking
and best learning practice to a global market.

Under a range of leading imprints, including
Financial Times Prentice Hall, we create world-class
print publications and electronic products giving readers
knowledge and understanding which can then be
applied, whether studying or at work.

To find out more about our business and professional
products, you can visit us at www.business-minds.com

For other Pearson Education publications, visit
www.pearsoned-ema.com

Pearson
Education

CAPTURING CUSTOMERS' HEARTS

Leave your competition to chase their pockets

BRIAN CLEGG

FINANCIAL TIMES

Prentice Hall

An imprint of Pearson Education

London • New York • San Francisco • Toronto • Sydney

Tokyo • Singapore • Hong Kong • Cape Town • Madrid

Paris • Milan • Munich • Amsterdam

PEARSON EDUCATION LIMITED

Head Office:
Edinburgh Gate
Harlow CM20 2JE
Tel: +44 (0)1279 623623
Fax: +44 (0)1279 431059

London Office:
128 Long Acre
London WC2E 9AN
Tel: +44 (0)20 7447 2000
Fax: +44 (0)20 7240 5771
Website: www.business-minds.com

First published in Great Britain in 2000

© Brian Clegg 2000

The right of Brian Clegg to be identified as Author
of this work has been asserted by him in accordance
with the Copyright, Designs and Patents Act 1988.

ISBN 0 273 649310

British Library Cataloguing in Publication Data
A CIP catalogue record for this book can be obtained from the British Library

10 9 8 7 6 5 4 3 2

Designed by Claire Brodmann Book Designs, Burton-on-Trent
Typeset by Northern Phototypesetting Co Ltd, Bolton
Printed and bound in Great Britain by Biddles Ltd, Guildford & King's Lynn

The Publishers' policy is to use paper manufactured from sustainable forests.

CONTENTS

ABOUT THE AUTHOR

With MAs in Natural Sciences (Cambridge) and Operational Research (Lancaster), Brian Clegg first worked in the Operational Research department of British Airways. After 17 years in the corporate world, specializing in finding new and innovative ways of using computers and information to benefit business, he established himself as a freelance writer and set up Creativity Unleashed Limited, a company specializing in consultancy on business creativity and customer service.

Brian Clegg is a regular contributor to *Professional Manager, Personal Computer World, Computer Weekly* and the world wide web-based magazine, *V3*. Among over 15 business titles, he has written *Imagination Engineering, DisOrganization* (both with Paul Birch), *The Chameleon Manager, Creativity and Innovation for Managers, Mining the Internet, Instant Time Management, Instant Stress Management, The Invisible Customer* and *Training Plus*.

PREFACE

Customer service has been a crucial focus for at least 15 years now. Does this mean that we can put our feet up, say 'we've done the customer' and move onto the next big thing? Not a chance. The continued focus on customers is an imperative given the realities of the marketplace:

- Good customer service is still the exception, even after all this time. Okay, the staff may have 'How can I help you?' on their name badges, and may have learned how to smile, but the service still stops a long way short of excellence.

- The customers' ideas of good service have been transformed in the last 15 years. The rise of consumerism and consumer rights attests to this – our customers expect more now. Much more.

- The opposition has not stayed still. If our relationship with our customers is to be a prime driver of differentiation, it is necessary to take a whole step further into customer satisfaction.

Survey after survey has shown that customers are deeply unhappy with service levels. When I was gathering stories to illustrate this book, it was very easy to get examples of bad customer service – but many, many people could not think of a *single* instance of great customer service. To make the customer

❝The continued focus on customers is an imperative given the realities of the marketplace.❞

relationship the driving force behind repeat business and differentiation calls for a quantum shift. From consumer friendliness to charisma. We don't want to be nice to our customers, we want them to love us. To desire our company's products. To speak to other people about our company with awe in their voices. We need to capture their hearts.

The cynical response is, 'It's nice if you can fake it.' But this isn't about faking it. *Capturing Customers' Hearts* looks at companies where the product or the company itself generates a special reaction in the customer, something much more than brand loyalty – true affection. You will never look at your customers in the same way again.

> 66 To make the customer relationship the driving force behind repeat business and differention calls for a quantum shift. From consumer friendliness to charisma. 99

ACKNOWLEDGEMENTS

Thanks to everyone at Pearson Education who have kept this going – particularly Pradeep Jethi and Richard Stagg. And a particular thank you to the customers who have provided examples, good and bad, including Elie Ball, Sean Berner, Paul Birch, Ian Burrell, Gregor Cosgrove, Adrian Critchlow, Mark Daymond, Kathryn Dodington, Jessica Figueras, David Freemantle, Nick Gassman, Rosie Greaves, John Harris, Philip Joisce, Anita Kerrigan, Keith Lawson, Brian Martin, Paul McGeary, Amy Merrill, Graham Rawlinson, Tara Robison, Tim Robison, Helen Rowlands and David Weeks.

CAPTURING HEARTS

An outstanding customer relationship is the only safe way of building differentiation. Companies with charisma are able to capture their customers' hearts – and that means holding onto customers when competition is at its most cruel.

THE TRUTH IS OUT THERE

The facts about customers are stark. They are as simple as A, B, C:

A   Businesses *need* customers. That's where the money comes from.

B   Businesses need to *attract* customers. That means having something the customers want. That 'something' is not just products and services, but the whole experience of dealing with your company.

C   Businesses need to *keep* customers. It costs much less to retain a customer than to get a new one – and losing existing customers means losing all that lifetime value. Big money in some cases.

This is stuff you learned at your mother's knee, right? Bear with me. So which of these scenarios is more likely to help attract and retain customers?

1   Your staff are rude. They ignore customers. When they do get round to providing service they are surly and clearly regard it a waste of their precious time. If something goes wrong, tough – they play it by the rules.

2   Your staff smile a lot. They go out of their way to help customers. They are really interested in the customers and what the customers want. When things go wrong they will do whatever is necessary to sort things out.

More idiot stuff. It's not exactly a difficult choice. So why is it that survey after survey at the end of the 1990s found decreases in customer satisfaction? Why is it that customer service is considered to be in decline? Why is that we all have plenty of stories of being badly treated by companies? Why is it that consumer rights shows are so popular on the TV? You get the point. We all know how important customers are. We all realize what will help build a good relationship with our customers. Yet so often it is done badly. So, if your

❝The facts about customers are stark. They are as simple as A, B, C.❞

> **❝Why is it that survey after survey at the end of the 1990s found decreases in customer satisfaction?❞**

company happens to be the one that gets it right, there's a big opportunity. A huge opportunity.

Because unlike great products, unlike low prices, great customer service is hard to copy. Differentiation is the name of the game.

WHAT ABOUT QUALITY?

Quality is wonderful. Delivering the right product to the right place at the right time is essential. That's one of the basics of business. But it is not enough when others can do the same. Quality is one of those sad attributes that is a real problem if it is missing, but isn't feted when it's there. If quality is absent – if you have consistently bad products or consistently late delivery – it won't matter how good your customer service is, the customers will become unhappy and start looking elsewhere. But quality alone isn't enough to retain the customers. You need something more.

WHY OKAY ISN'T GOOD ENOUGH

As we will examine more in the next chapter, we have all done customer service. Many companies have even got it to a level that could be described as passable. They have provided their customer contact staff with scripts that are welcoming. They have made the level of service consistent across their outlets. They have made the experience of dealing with the company pleasant, in a bland sort of way. Surely they can tick the 'customer service' box and get on to some real business?

Surely not. Customer service is going through the same sort of cycle as the development of industry, but way behind. This type of pre-packaged customer service corresponds to the production line. Production line customer service enabled us to spread good customer service widely and cheaply where it was not available before. But there are drawbacks. Just like the production line, such

> 66 Unlike great products, unlike low prices, great customer service is hard to copy. 99

> 66 We have all done customer service. Many companies have even got it to a level that could be described as passable. 99

customer service tends to demoralize the workforce and produces bland, repetitious product. It's a delight when you're used to nothing, but it doesn't compare to the real, hand-made thing.

You might have statistics that you think disprove this. Ninety-five per cent (or however many) of your customers are 'quite satisfied' with your service, so it seems that there is no need for action. But be very wary.

BUILDING CHARISMA

The interesting thing about customer service is that it is often driven by perception. A company's reputation for service (or lack of it) is often built up from a series of small experiences from which people generalize. Very few of us are able to generate the total picture from which we can form a completely objective opinion. We are driven by our 'feel' for a company based on our inevitably limited anecdotal experiences.

David Freemantle, consultant and author of
Superboss and *What Customers Like About You*

David Freemantle highlights the disaster of believing your own statistics. Customers don't know (or care) about your statistics. Their view of your company is predicated on the stories they hear, the collection of individual experiences they build. It is each individual story that will make the difference, not the statistics.

Those stories aren't generated by passable customer service. They need something more to kick them into life. It's time to give our businesses charisma.

66Ninety-five per cent (or however many) of your customers are 'quite satisfied' with your service, so it seems that there is no need for action. But be very wary.99

66Customers don't know (or care) about your statistics. Their view of your company is predicated on the stories they hear, the collection of individual experiences they build.99

CHARISMA

Charisma is about inspiration. It is the property of a person that inspires enthu-siasm, interest or affection in others. It is attractive. In fact, it's just what a business needs to take those customers beyond service, beyond a relationship or an experience. A business with charisma gives the customer something very special. When you've dealt with a business with charisma, you want to tell others about it. You want to share your feelings. If we can imbue a business with charisma, we have something that has the brightness of a searchlight alongside the candle flame of everyday customer service. This book is about giving your business charisma.

TAKE IT FROM HERE

The remainder of the book is a guide to the components that make up charisma in a business. The next chapter looks at the nature of conventional customer service, at its benefits and limitations. From there we explore the 12 charisma components, from going the extra light year to the strange twelfth component.

1 GOING THE EXTRA LIGHT YEAR

In a way, this first component pulls all the others together. It's an attractive trait if someone goes out of their way to help you. Equally, it's attractive if a company goes that extra mile. But for true charisma, to stand out like a beacon, you have to do more – to go the extra light year, the first component of capturing customers' hearts.

❝Charisma is about inspiration... When you've dealt with a business with charisma, you want to tell others about it.❞

2 IF IT'S BROKE, FIX IT

We all get it wrong sometimes. Zero defect is a fantasy beloved of quality circles, but it is not a fact of human life. However good our systems and procedures and staff, things will go wrong – and then the customer measures the company's worth on how well we fix things. All too often, service recovery is grudging, set about with conditions and rules that make the hard-done-by customer feel like a criminal. If this is how you treat your customers, you are missing a huge opportunity for building up charisma.

3 I'M IN LOVE WITH MY CAR

There are some products and brands that produce in the customer a reaction wildly disproportionate to their nominal value. It's true of some cars, for instance, which have an almost fanatical following. Often these aren't the best products by any conventional measure – instead they have a certain quirkiness that seems to generate such affection. You can't engineer a product to be charismatic, but you can encourage it in that direction – and make sure that you maintain the benefit once you have a product that has achieved this status.

4 THEY KNOW ME

The whole field of customer relationship management (CRM) has built up around the thesis that you can give customers a better experience if you know about them and make use of that knowledge in the way you serve them. Unfortunately, CRM has all too often been driven by systems (and systems manufacturers) rather than the realities of human relationships. But this shouldn't be allowed to cloud the reality that the company that really makes the customer feel recognized and welcome has a big stake in the charisma game.

❝Zero defect is a fantasy beloved of quality circles, but it is not a fact of human life.❞

❝There are some products and brands that produce in the customer a reaction wildly disproportionate to their nominal value.❞

5 STAR POWER

Companies who don't have a star figurehead tend to be cynical about those who do. The key figures are regarded as unrepentant self-publicists for whom the limelight is more important than the success of the business. Yet this overlooks the fact that the members of public like a recognizable human face for a company. You can't identify with a corporation – you can with a famous chief executive. For that matter, you can with any famous employee – or maybe the whole team.

Perhaps everyone can be a star.

6 THEY'RE PEOPLE LIKE US

As a gross generalization, people like people. They like dealing with real people. They have relationships with real people, not with companies. So the more it is possible to make your customer contact staff into real people, the better. That means staff who behave like people, not like automata. It means real people with real enthusiasms – especially those that are shared with the customers. And it means people we have to trust to get it right. There can be no charisma from staff in a straitjacket.

7 SURPRISE, SURPRISE!

Dullness and charisma don't go together. Once upon a time, consistency was a customer service god, but if everything is the same, if everything is predictable, there can be no excitement, no charisma. The element of surprise, provided it

66Perhaps everyone can be a star.99

66The element of surprise, provided it is a pleasant surprise, is a key component to keeping your customers intrigued and coming back for more.99

is a pleasant surprise, is a key component to keeping your customers intrigued and coming back for more. Don't bore them until they run over to the competition – keep the creativity and fun flowing.

8 TECHNICAL WIZARDRY

It's often said that men don't really grow up – they remain enthralled by toys for their whole life. Whether your customers are men or women, technical flair will appeal to their male side. Sometimes charisma needs a little gloss – used correctly, technical polish is a valuable addition.

Technology also needs to be optional – some customers are turned off by it – but for many it is an effective attractor.

9 THEY'RE MINE, ALL MINE

To call someone parochial is usually an insult, and yet we all have a degree of positive parochialism. It doesn't matter if it's my town, my country or my football team – we like to see our own do well. The more we can bring customers to feel that they own the company, the more they will feel inseparable from the company and its fortunes. Make the company theirs and loyalty is no longer an issue – it's a fait accompli.

10 CUTE AND CUDDLY

If technology appeals to the male in us all, there's something about being cute and cuddly that tugs at our female side. To be charismatic is not necessarily to be loveable, but companies that give their customers that warm glow are inevitably charismatic.

66 Make the company theirs and loyalty is no longer an issue – it's a fait accompli. 99

66 To be charismatic is not necessarily to be loveable, but companies that give their customers that warm glow are inevitably charismatic. 99

11 WE KEEP IN TOUCH

Communication is at the heart of human relationships and is equally important in fostering the relationship between a human being and a company. So often the things that go wrong are a result of a breakdown in communications. Keeping up a dialogue and making it obvious that you enjoy that communication makes it difficult for a customer to resist. You should never let up on communication.

12 THE TWELFTH COMPONENT

That's 11 out of the way, but what of the twelfth? I have to confess that consideration of a twelfth component arose initially out of a sense of order. There's something lumpy and unsatisfactory about the number 11, compared to the serried order of 12. When I began to think about what a twelfth component could be, I realized it was just as well that I had undertaken the exercise, because I had missed something big. Most people would accept that some companies have attributes that make the unique. What I came to realize, however, is that this statement can be generalized. Every company has its unique attributes, and these form the twelfth component that can bring charisma.

But before launching into the components, what are things like now? After all, everyone has done customers, haven't they?

66 Communication is at the heart of human relationships... You should never let up on communication. 99

66 Every company has its unique attributes, and these form the twelfth component that can bring charisma. 99

WE'VE DONE CUSTOMERS

Previous customer service pushes have run down and lost energy, leaving customer care often well supported by lip service and less so by practice. The realities of customer relations at the start of the 21st century are often less than desirable. Even where there is a company standard, the result is often artificial and second-best.

WE'VE SEARCHED FOR EXCELLENCE

In theory, the closing 20 years of the 20th century should have been the years when customer service flourished. There was certainly enough talked about it. When Tom Peters and his co-authors wrote the *Excellence* books, they prompted a whole new attitude to customer service. What had often been seen as a necessary evil was moved to the centre of many businesses' attention. There was a genuine new enthusiasm, at least at managerial levels, for a focus on the customer and the customer's need.

It was just as well. Peters might have found some companies that seemed to get it right, but there were plenty of examples of mediocrity. In part, this was possible because of the post-war boom, when the new prosperity in the West had fuelled a consumer bonanza. It didn't really matter what your service was like; people would snatch the goods from your hands. The mere novelty of fast food, for instance, was enough, without worrying too much about the service. But by the 1980s there was a need for something more. The consumer had become more sophisticated. The few competitors that had latched onto customer service as a route to differentiation were beginning to cash in on their daring. The signs were all there.

WE'VE PUT PEOPLE FIRST

Some companies made a huge turnaround on customer service. A classic example would be the international airline, British Airways. In the early 1980s, recently formed from the shattered remains of two long-underfunded nation-

66 Peters and his co-authors prompted a whole new attitude to customer service. 99

66 The few competitors that had latched onto customer service as a route to differentiation were beginning to cash in on their daring. 99

alized carriers, British Airways was in a bad way. The staff had a reputation for coldness; dealing with the airline still felt like coping with a state bureaucracy. You flew with BA because you had to, not because you wanted to.

New chief executive, Colin Marshall, brought in from Avis to turn the company around, saw the opportunity for change. He introduced a massive programme to drag the airline over to a customer focus. Every member of staff went through a one-day session called 'Putting People First' that emphasized the importance of people to business survival, where 'people' included both customers and staff. Each of these days was closed by a question and answer session, almost all of which were attended by Marshall himself. It was all about a change of mindset, moving the employees from seeing themselves as responsible for moving metal tubes through the air, to seeing themselves as responsible for giving the customer an enjoyable experience.

Business boomed. The airline became one of the few to make consistent profits. It won enough awards to christen itself 'The World's Favourite Airline'. Marshall's team continued with a series of sessions for all staff and for managers, reinforcing the customer message. There's no doubt at all that the campaign was a great success.

So with companies like BA putting people first, and a wider acknowledgement of the need for excellence, is there any point in banging the customer service drum again? Hasn't it all been done? Unfortunately, the answer is a resounding no. Four problems have stopped the customer service revolution from continuing to blossom in the 21st century:

- consumer expectation
- the rundown
- lip service
- sudden growth.

❝In the early 1980s British Airways was in a bad way.❞

THE NEW CONSUMER EXPECTATION

All the factors blocking customer service success are people issues. To begin with, the customers themselves are changing. As electronic communications and the media pump more and more information around the global marketplace, consumer awareness of what is possible is at a new height. Consumers expect an awful lot more than they did only a few years ago. A wider experience of the world has given us broader comparisons. The popularity of consumer TV programmes has made it more natural to notice and complain when things go wrong. We are consciously on the lookout for service failure.

In fact, things don't even have to go wrong to get the thumbs down. When US fast food restaurants were introduced to the UK they took the country by storm. Used to dingy cafés with surly staff who took an age to produce a grey, greasy burger, the UK was wowed by the speed, consistency and friendliness of companies like McDonald's and Burger King. But now that these brand names are a normal and expected part of the high street, there is a desire for something more. We know what a fast food company does – that's the bare minimal expectation. To be outstanding, we want the next generation.

If a company is to hold on to customers, to reap the benefits of the customer's lifetime value, it has to reflect this change and go beyond mere customer service. The new models are building a relationship and giving the customer an experience. A satisfied customer is not just looking for the right product at the right time and the right price. They want pleasure, they want thrill, they want the glow that dealing with your company can give. The

❝All factors blocking customer service success are people issues.❞

❝We are consciously on the lookout for service failure.❞

chapters that follow detail 12 different components of this glow. To an extent this is a menu. It might be possible to pick and choose between the components. But bear in mind that the winning companies will be those that can provide their customers with a free-choice buffet offering the whole range of options.

THE RUNDOWN

Many of the companies that did take action on customer service, such as British Airways, are now finding things tougher. Not only has the commercial environment changed – things have never before been this competitive – but customer service is one of those strange, Lewis Carroll-like topics where you have to run just to stand still. Too many companies assumed that they had 'done' customer service and could now leave that to tick over while they concentrated on other areas of urgent need. Unfortunately, when left alone, customer service doesn't tick over, it runs down.

Many companies that had a customer service push are now suffering from a backlash. New people have come into the organization, people who weren't

A satisfied customer is not just looking for the right product at the right time and the right price.

The winning companies will be those that can provide their customers with a free-choice buffet.

Things have never before been this competitive.

Many companies that had a customer service push are now suffering from a backlash.

there when the culture was built. New pressures, products and services make it harder for the staff to continue with the focus on customer service. Cost-cutting drives nibble away at the service levels. After a while a strange form of laziness sets in. No one likes to do the same thing all the time – even when it's a basic like being nice to people, it starts to pall. All too often, companies that have made a customer service push in the past are finding themselves in real danger over an issue that they thought was conquered.

LIP SERVICE

But at least those companies did try. The worst case of customer service failure is lip service – and frighteningly it seems to be the most common. While practically every company did latch onto customer service in the 1980s and 1990s, and put grandiose statements concerning the importance of customer service into their literature, too often talking about it was all they managed to do. It was almost as if customer service was considered a sort of magic – you only had to mention it to fix the problems.

Such companies frequently didn't think through the implications of improving customer service. They weren't happy to take on the cost that customer service carries, even though it brings with it immense benefits of customer retention. They didn't see the need to change the company culture, thinking it was enough to tell the customer contact staff that they should give better service. Most of all, managers weren't prepared to let go. Unless the front line staff have the ability to take action to serve customers without resorting to procedures and chains of authority there can be no true customer service. For many managers this was giving too much leeway to staff they didn't trust. Result – customers didn't get service, they got a bureaucracy.

❝Unless the front line staff have the ability to take action to serve customers without resorting to procedures and chains of authority there can be no true customer service.❞

HORROR STORY

TAKEN TO THE CLEANERS

A representative of a nationwide chain of clothing cleaners appeared on a TV consumer affairs show, defending his company against customer complaints. 'Customer service is very important to us,' he said. 'We have millions of garments brought in and very few complaints. If anyone has a problem they only need to pay for the cause of the damage to be verified by an independent assessor, and we'll compensate them in full if we're proved to be at fault.'

This was a bizarre statement. How could the executive from the cleaning company suggest with a straight face that customer service was very important to his company? If there were only a few complaints, why didn't they assume that the customer was in the right? Under such circumstances it seems ridiculous that anyone should be made to prove, at their own expense, that the company had made a mistake. It would be terrifying to do business with a company that *didn't* think customer service was important if this was an example of one that did.

SUDDEN GROWTH

One blockage to good customer service arose out of the technological changes in this period. Particularly in the IT field, companies were springing out of nothing and becoming enormous in immensely compressed timescales. The PC and then the Internet hit business with an unparalleled force. Growth was unbelievably fast. As a result of this, companies whose business has been driven by the PC or the Internet have been in a unique position. It really hasn't mattered what their customer service was like – they just had to concentrate on getting product out of the door quickly enough, such was demand.

H O R R O R   S T O R Y

THE LATE BASKET

E-tailers, selling over the Internet, have often suffered from the inability to set up proper service channels in time to keep up with their sudden arrival on the scene. Take this painful example. A company ordered a gift for a client from an online store we'll call pressies.com (if at some future date a 'pressies.com' is set up, there wasn't one at the time of writing). It was a Christmas gift, ordered well before the holidays for delivery on Christmas Eve. After the event, the following string of e-mails passed between pressies.com and the customer. They are repro- duced here to get the full flavour of how the interaction was mismanaged.

From: Pressies.com Customer Service
Sent: Wednesday, January 12, 2000 9:37 AM
To: Hilary

Hilary,

The executive basket that you ordered is no longer available, due to technical issues with the vender. We can send either a dried fruit basket or a deluxe exotic fruit basket. We will be able to ship these priority with no additional charge to you.

We would like to hear from you as soon as possible to get this order processed and delivered.

When you contact us, please make to the attention of the escalation dept. to expedite this for you.

Thank you for your patience in this matter.

Fred X
Escalation Team, pressies.com

From: Clarissa

Sent: Friday, January 14, 2000 3:50 AM

To: Pressies.Com Customer Service

Dear Customer Services @ pressies.com

I am responding to your email on behalf of my colleague, Hilary, who is just too furious to reply herself.

We are both severely disappointed that you failed to send the hamper we ordered.

Informing us on the 12th January, 3 weeks after the hamper was supposed to have reached its destination, that the hamper was no longer in stock is not good enough as far as we are concerned. We appreciate that you must have been busy, but in the world that we live in, a speedy response is very important.

We will be refusing to foot the bill for this one, and think that you should send the recipient a basket of exotic fruit, free of charge, by way of an apology AND in the name of maintaining good customer relations.

Did I mention that we are in the business of media/journalism and will not hesitate to air our views to the public about the level of your service, or lack thereof, as the case may be.

I look forward to your response

Clarissa

From: Pressies.com Customer Service
Sent: Friday, January 14, 2000 2:33 PM
To: Hilary; Clarissa

Dear Hilary/Clarissa,

We are going to ship this out on Monday for overnight delivery. We will credit your account for the full amount of the purchase. We really are sorry that you have had such a poor experience with us but we are a new site and just in the second phase of a three phase roll out. We are trying to correct all the problems and will have then fixed in the near future. We would hope that you would be patient with us and visit our site again and give us another chance to keep you as a customer.

We would like to give you a coupon code for future use on another order. This coupon will give you $15 off the order. If for some reason this doesn't work please contact us and we will give you another one to try.

Thank you for shopping Pressies.com

Sally

From: Pressies.com Customer Service

Sent: Wednesday, January 19, 2000 1:01 AM

To: Hilary

Dear Hilary

The following item shipped today:

Order Number: 123456

1 – Executive Basket

Thank you for your business!!

Sincerely,

Pressies.com Customer Service

From: Hilary

Sent: Wednesday, January 19, 2000 2:53 AM

To: Pressies.Com Customer Service

I'm a bit confused re this.

Is this being delivered free of charge as stated in your email to Clarry and myself. If this is not the case, I no longer wish this to be delivered seeing as it was supposed to be delivered before Xmas. It seems a bit pointless now nearly a month later.

Please advise.

Regards

Hilary

From: support@pressies.com
Sent: Wednesday, January 19, 2000 2:15 PM
To: Hilary

Dear Hilary

This was delivered on 1/18/00 at 2:57PM the tracking information is below.

We didn't charge you any shipping on this item. You will still see a charge for the basket. Since this has been delivered already we can't cancel the order.

Thank you for shopping Pressies.com

Sally

From: Hilary
Sent: Wednesday, January 19, 2000 2:19 PM
To: Pressies.Com Customer Service

I will not be paying for the basket since it was clearly stated in Clarissa's first piece of correspondence with you – and I quote:

We will be refusing to foot the bill for this one, and think that you should send the recipient a basket of exotic fruit, free of charge, by way of an apology AND in the name of maintaining good customer relations.

This was in no way at all a command for you to send the basket anyway and then charge us for it. It was merely a suggestion, and perhaps a lesson, in good customer relations. I would say that sending a basket nearly a month late and then charge for this service is a complete joke and a further insult to injury.

You clearly stated in your correspondence to Clarissa and myself the following:

We are going to ship this out on Monday for overnight delivery. We will credit your account for the full amount of the purchase.

▶

Now forgive me if I'm wrong, but the above does not refer JUST to the shipping costs, it clearly states that my account will be reimbursed for the full amount of the purchase – that means I should receive a COMPLETE refund.

You then go on to say that:

We would hope that you would be patient with us and visit our site again and give us another chance to keep you as a customer.

I can safely say that I will not be using your site in either the near or distant future, and I will certainly not be recommending your service to any of my colleagues or friends.

In future I suggest that you keep a detailed record of what you promise to every disgruntled customer and ensure that your promises are fulfilled as it only heightens the anger, disgust and frustration. I cannot communicate my displeasure enough to you – I can't believe that in a world where Internet services are springing up every second, that you are risking the future of your company with such poor customer relations.

I expect full confirmation that a refund has been actioned and the contact name and details of where I can lodge an official complaint.

Looking forward to a speedy response.

Best wishes

Hilary

From: support@pressies.com
Sent: Thursday, January 20, 2000 10:25 AM
To: Hilary

Dear Hilary/Clarissa,

We are giving you full credit for this item. We are sorry for the confusion on this matter. You should see a credit on your card in the future. This process could take up to 3 weeks to process.

Thank you for shopping pressies.com

Sally

The inability to recognize the needs of the customer illustrated in the pressies.com story is the sign of an immature industry. But there are some indicators that maturity is coming to the field, and even those companies that have achieved immense success by going around customer service rather than by providing it (dare we mention Microsoft?) will have to watch their backs very soon. Sudden growth is exciting, but it is also dangerous.

THE GAP

The outcome of these four factors is a widening gap between customer expectations and the actuality companies are delivering. Often a company is suffering from a combination of the factors, making customer service even more of a

66 Sudden growth is exciting, but it is also dangerous. 99

66 Most large companies have taken only the first trembling steps in the direction of good customer service. 99

problem. It seems odd that something apparently so well understood remains such a barrier, but in fact most large companies have taken only the first trembling steps in the direction of good customer service.

HORROR STORY

BANKING ON IT

Banks are increasingly relying on telephone and online support for their customers, but some banks still give the impression that they believe customers owe them a living.

My business bank account is managed at a branch around 50 miles away from my business. When my business relocated, it wasn't worth all the paperwork required to change branch – or so it seemed at the time. Quite often we don't get around to writing the cheque to transfer our own salaries from the company into our personal accounts – instead we phone up the bank and ask for a transfer.

A month or so ago I rang the bank. I described to the agent what I wanted to do. 'It's not possible,' she said. 'I'm not authorized to do it.' I pointed out that I had been doing it on and off for the last three years. 'Who did it for you?' she asked, 'because we aren't allowed to do it.' I was puzzled. How should I know who had done it? 'Whoever answered the phone did it,' I replied. 'They can't have,' she said, 'they aren't authorized to.' By now I was getting angry. 'You can look on my statements. It has been done.'

The agent persisted with the line that an agent like her would not be able to make the transfer. I would have to have dealt with the manager – and he probably wouldn't do it. I was faced with this information, set against the fact that I had done the same transaction over the phone with the agent that answered it at least half a dozen times before. What the agent seemed to be saying was that I was lying. I was not happy. It was quite acceptable that as a security precaution the bank made it difficult to transfer money out (although a modern bank should have had appropriate mechanisms), but it was entirely wrong that the agent should suggest (whether or not consciously) that I was lying.

66 Some banks still give the impression that they believe

customers owe them a living. 99

This gap between expectations and reality is not entirely bad news. For the company that is prepared to do something about it, the gap means that customer service remains a stunningly powerful opportunity for differentiation. If you can get customer service right, and continue to enhance it, you can overtake customer expectations, cease living in the past, move away from lip service and overcome the dangers of explosive development. What is needed is a new construction kit to build customer service – which the 12 components of this book provide.

WHO ARE YOUR CUSTOMERS ANYWAY?

When thinking about customer service, you always need to have in the back of your mind the question of the customers' identity. All too often we assume that our customers are just the people who currently pay us money. There is a need to take a wider view. What about your immediate customers' bosses or families? What about the people who *could* buy your products and services, but who are spending their money elsewhere? It is instructive that luxury car manufacturer Mercedes-Benz considers its competitors at the top end of the market to include manufacturers of helicopters and yachts. We're used to competitor analysis, but we need to make sure we also keep an eye on those competitors' customers. For that matter, what about your suppliers – aren't they potential customers with a vested interest in your company doing well?

> **"Customer service remains a stunningly powerful opportunity for differentiation. If you can get customer service right, you can overtake customer expectations."**

> **"What about the people who *could* buy your products and services, but who are spending their money elsewhere?"**

> **"It is instructive that luxury car manufacturer Mercedes-Benz considers its competitors at the top end of the market to include manufacturers of helicopters and yachts."**

GOOD NEWS STORY

PUTTING ON THE SHINE

A director of an international pharmaceutical company was travelling across the Atlantic with a major airline. The pharmaceutical company had an agreement with the airline to provide all their air travel – a deal that was beneficial to both of them. The director opened his first class washbag and noticed that the toothpaste was made by a competitor. He did a quick calculation. The revenue his company brought to the airline was at least ten times the cost of the products in the bag. On his return to the office, he brought this discrepancy to the notice of the board of the airline. Within a month, the airline had changed its supplier to the pharmaceutical company.

This isn't a book about identifying customers and potential customers – that's a whole blockbuster in its own right – but it is important when looking at the components of charisma to consider not only those that will appeal to your perceived current customer base but also to potential customers and influencers. Note particularly those influencers. It has taken a long time, but retailers are gradually realizing how much family members influence the traditionally nominated decision maker in the choice of a product. It might be children influencing a PC purchase, husbands fascinated by white goods with clever gizmos or wives choosing the family car – or a whole different range of broken stereotypes – the fact is that your aim should be to influence the people who are likely to make the decision to spend with you, or to spend with you again. They are the people whose hearts you need to capture. Time to switch on the charm.

66 Your aim should be to influence the people who are likely to make the decision to spend with you, or to spend with you again. 99

66 Time to switch on the charm. 99

1

GOING THE EXTRA LIGHT YEAR

For a long time 'going the extra mile' has been the winning formula. But the mile has been eroded, forcing companies to go a lot further to demonstrate charisma. It is even necessary to consider the radical step of giving customers what they want, and all this without breaking the bank.

GOING THE EXTRA MILE

We are all impressed by achievements that stretch an individual to the limit. Our imaginations are captured by record breakers, or by walks across the ice to the South Pole, or successful climbs of vast mountains. The stretching involved makes these feats more interesting than someone who ran for a bus once, someone who walked to the ice-cream parlour, or someone who climbed a small hill. Similarly, we are impressed when a company or an individual working for that company makes the effort to go beyond expectations on our behalf.

This is where the first big problem comes with traditional training or customer service standards, manuals and scripts. As soon as the member of staff is doing their job, following the rules, keeping to standards they aren't pushing the boundary – they are just doing the standard job, like the fast food server who hopes that you have a nice day (and would you like any sauce with that?)

HORROR STORY

THE USELESS PLUMBER

'A week or two ago, on a Saturday (of course!) our central heating stopped. I could tell that it was not the boiler that was at fault as the hot water was. (Hot that is.)

'I tried to ring our usual plumber – no reply. I then rang a firm that we had used in the distant past. I described the symptoms.

'"Ah yes sir, that will be the thermostat in the boiler." I repeated that the water was being heated and that their diagnosis just *might* be mistaken. Their reply was along the lines of – leave the plumbing to plumbers. Before I could say anything more on that I was told their charges – high – and that they could possibly fit me in as an emergency (bearing in mind the frost on the ground outside) the following Tuesday. I declined.

'We have gas fires and heaters and managed reasonably comfortably until Monday morning when I rang my plumber again. He agreed with my diagnosis of a faulty valve, was somewhat taken aback when I could give him not only the make but the model number, and then said "The only trouble is, I'm due in Plymouth this afternoon." But then went on to say that if I could be home from the office within the hour he would drop in on his way. I could and he did. He was in and out of the house within 15 minutes!'

The bad plumber in this story was not only unprepared to go the extra mile, he didn't even know how to start. One of the reasons customer satisfaction is at an overall low is because of this couldn't care less attitude, all too typical of many companies.

THE DEVALUED MILE

Much that has been done in the name of customer service standards has devalued going the extra mile, turning it into a bland, pasteurized parody of the real thing. That is why I am suggesting we need to go the extra light year. To get beyond the morass of standardized, off-the-shelf customer service, we need to scramble up more than head and shoulders above the rest – by a whole order of magnitude.

This is a real problem that tends to be ignored. The whole look-alike, customer friendly movement now does more harm than good. A lapel badge saying 'I'm Molly, Have a nice day' can actually have a negative effect on customer service. The assumption is that you can take existing poor standards and pin on the appearance of caring – then all will be well. In fact, thanks to the devaluation that has taken place you would be much better off stripping out the whole mechanism and replacing it with something new.

Much contemporary customer service is in the same position as gas lighting companies when electric lights were just being introduced. Instead of getting into electric lighting, most gas light companies tried bringing out better or cheaper gas lamps to overcome the new competition. It didn't work. The same thing is happening with the gas light equivalent of customer service. The answer isn't more of the same, it is something new.

DISTANCE CAN BE RELATIVE

Bear in mind when attempting to do more than go the extra mile that distance in this sense is a relative concept.

66 Much that has been done in the name of customer service standards has devalued going the extra mile, turning it into a bland pasteurized parody of the real thing. 99

66 The answer isn't more of the same, it is something new. 99

GOOD NEWS STORY

THE AMERICAN DREAM

This US resident was born in the UK, giving him a particularly useful perspective on customer service.

'I live in the land of great customer service. It was hard to get used to. "Can I help you?" the second you walk into any store used to really annoy me; now if I haven't been asked within 20 seconds, I'm likely to leave. It's much easier to ask the assistant where things are than to browse around yourself. Which brings me to what happens when I come back to England.

'Service levels in UK supermarkets are so bad, it actually makes me laugh out loud while I'm in line. Here they are almost fighting to serve you. They have people wandering the aisles in case you need help finding something. I have *never* left a US supermarket with anything other than everything I wanted.'

It would be easy, given this good news, for US stores to relax. They've already gone the distance, it seems. Yet it's not that simple. It's that sneaky word 'extra'. US customer service may be way ahead of its European equivalent, but that doesn't matter a damn if your competitors are other US stores. You still need to go the extra light year compared to the competition. The pressure is still on. Meanwhile, UK customer service has often not even reached the starting line.

BEWARE ACCOUNTANTS

Another reason not to get too complacent in the USA – as soon as you let your guard down the accountants are going to step in and spoil things. This has been illustrated with delightful fervour on domestic flights in the USA. At one time

❝US customer service may be way ahead of its European equivalent, but that doesn't matter a damn if your competitors are other US stores.❞

you used to be pretty well guaranteed a meal, peanuts with your drink and pleasant attention from the flight attendant. Now you are treated as an irritation that gets in the way of the smooth operation of the company.

Interestingly, some airlines have even used the classic argument that this was done because customers wanted it. Unfortunately, this argument totally ignores the nature of causality. The theory goes that people want cheap flights. We can make flights cheaper by removing all the frills. Therefore people want flights without frills. However, if you were merely to ask 'Would you like a flight with no food and surly attendants?', the chances are you would get a different reaction.

'People want it cheap' might be the accountants' mantra, but that isn't the same as 'people want it cheap at the expense of customer service'. Relatively few people actually want to pay excessive prices (though we all need to consider how to accommodate those who do), but most would rather pay a little more for a great experience, rather than struggle along with cheap and cheerless delivery. You've only got to look at the success of the Disney resorts to realize this.

GIVING THE GLOW

To go that extra light year, our customer contact staff need to give the customers a glow. To make the experience of dealing with them something special. We'll see plenty of specifics in the other components, but this glow can be put down to three things – what you say, how you say it and what you do. Trivial really. Surely anyone can be trained to say the right things, to say it with a smile and to do it in the right way? That's fine until you look at what we are asking of the staff.

Start with the 'doing it' bit. This comes down to asking staff to take the initiative. If something needs to be done on the customer's behalf, to go ahead and do it, rather than report a problem to whoever is responsible, or worse still

66'People want it cheap' might be the accounts' mantra.99

66To go that extra light year, our customer contact staff need to give the customers a glow.99

ignore it. I've lost count of the number of times I have seen little things awry in supermarkets or other stores. Items fallen on the floor. Price tags missing. Displaced displays and broken bulbs. And at the same time I have seen plenty of staff standing around in the same area, doing nothing about it. Why? Because it's not their job. Because they don't care.

GOOD NEWS STORY

DOCTOR, DOCTOR

'I recently attended our local surgery, a practice with five doctors on its lists. Due to a receptionist's error, I was left waiting longer than usual. One of the doctors (not the one I was waiting to see), noticed I had been sitting there a while and checked with the receptionist to make sure he shouldn't have seen me, waking them up to my presence.

'It's often a collection of little items like this that add up to going the extra light year – taking the trouble to check what is happening when you notice something unusual. Putting things right without being asked. Thanks, Doctor Muller.'

Experience has shown that it's not enough to establish a policy. Frankly, policies rarely achieve what they are designed to do. Like all rules, they restrict rather than free up for action. Instead you have to start with culture. There has to be a belief in the company that making things happen is down to *me* (whatever is required) and I'll sort it. And enjoy sorting it. This isn't something that you can achieve in a training session alone. It needs constant reinforcement – and that reinforcement won't get across until it works all the way up the ladder. Until the chief executive won't pass a broken light bulb without doing

Experience has shown that it's not enough to establish a policy.

something about it. Once the big boss has been seen sweeping up flour in aisle 23, or dropping everything to help a customer fill in a form – and been seen to do so by a large number of the staff – the message will start getting across.

This same from-the-top approach can be seen in how we communicate with customers. Is it entirely surprising that customer contact staff don't take customers' conversations, letters and e-mails too seriously if it is career suicide to send one e-mail to the CX? We have all been at service points where the agent finishes a conversation with someone else first, or works through a piece of paperwork before bothering to look up and acknowledge a customer. This sort of behaviour is simply not acceptable as customer service – yet it's a magnificent reflection of how many managers still treat their staff. Isn't there a lesson here somewhere?

The need to smile is also more elusive than it should be. Smiling at customers, being genuinely friendly to them, is Customer Service 101. There probably isn't a company in business that doesn't ask its customer service staff to smile at customers. So why is that we see so many expressions ranging from bored to miserable?

Interestingly, some unstructured research has suggested that many people don't even know what a surly expression they are presenting to the world. At worst they think they have a 'neutral' expression, at best a smile. The trouble is, neutral expressions aren't neutral at all. Next time you are in a restaurant or in a park or on a train – anywhere with plenty of other people at repose – have a look around. Most people look unhappy. They don't feel that way, but the natural, relaxed facial expression isn't positive. It gives the lie to all that guff about a smile needing fewer muscles than a frown.

In the end there are only two things that are going to get natural smiles onto the faces of your staff. One is to make it a habit, reinforced perhaps by oppor-

> 66 Once the big boss has been seen sweeping up flour in aisle 23... the message will start getting across. 99

> 66 The need to smile is more elusive than it should be. 99

> 66 Make smiles a conscious part of the uniform, backed up perhaps by a reward 99

tunities to see their faces in the workplace at regular intervals. The other is to get them to understand just how potent the expression is in giving the customer that special glow, and to make smiles a conscious part of the uniform, backed up perhaps by a reward.

Even the conversation that gives the glow is not easy to deal with. As soon as we are into scripts, we have lost the glow. It is fine for customer service staff to know the message that they need to get across, but if they can't do it in their own words, if they can't modify the content to match the individual customer, there is no way to give that glow. After all, no one could really pretend that they are putting themselves out for a customer, or giving them the impression of chatting to a friend, when they're really reciting a script.

GOOD NEWS STORY

CHECK THIS OUT

This example of the positive value of conversation took place at a supermarket checkout somewhere in New York State.

'A little while ago, in a small supermarket, I was at the checkout. The sales assistant paused as she put one of the items through the scanner. "That's cool," she said, "I haven't seen one of those before. They're amazing value, aren't they? I'll have to get one myself." It made me feel so good.'

Two things were happening here. The agent was indirectly complimenting the customer on her choice, and was giving an 'insider' view that the product was good value. The customer got a glow from this aside. There is a small risk in a high tech environment that the customer would be concerned that the agent didn't know about a product, but generally this approach (if not overused and made mechanical) will be very effective at giving the glow. Make sure, though, that the product is one that could genuinely elicit such a response. Being apparently pleasantly surprised about the existence of a common everyday item ('Gee, a paperclip – what a neat idea') or gushing about a new product that simply isn't inspiring ('Isn't this brilliant? Having an extra slice of ham in the packet – I'd never have thought of that. I must get some myself') is immediately false and destroys the illusion of having a genuine conversation.

THE STUPID AND THE DIFFICULT

It's all very well aspiring to give the customers something special, to go beyond expectations, but sometimes it seems that the customer is just too stupid or intentionally difficult to manage this. Most customer service staff have some story to tell of difficult customers.

HORROR STORY

MR ANGRY

This story, in an agent's own words, is from a call centre in Dallas, Texas. It is all too typical of the irrational behaviour that customer service staff have to cope with. The conversation revolves around a modem, a device used to connect PCs to the Internet, and an Internet service provider (ISP). At the time, a popular type of modem was labelled 56k, suggesting that it could handle 56,000 bits per second (actually 57,344 bits per second, but let's not be fussy). As John, the agent at the ISP, tells the customer, this was not the reality.

Phone rings…

Me: This is John, how may I help you?

Customer: I have a 56k modem, but I only connect at 45,333. Are you guys having some kind of problem?

Me: No, sir, that's not a problem; that's about an average connect speed.

Customer: What do you mean an average connect speed? What's the problem over there? When are you going to upgrade your equipment?

Me: Sir, we have state-of-the-art 56k equipment. It's made by Nortel. FCC regulations prevent you from connecting at a full 56k. Not only that but the technology is limited by the quality of your phone lines.

Customer: Well, there's nothing wrong with my phone line!

Me: You must have a perfectly clean line to get a significantly higher connection speed. Very few people have such a line.

▶

Customer: My friend across the street connects to his ISP at 57,600. I think you guys need to get it together up there.

Me: Sir, that speed that he is seeing is not the speed at which he is connecting to his ISP, that's the speed that his computer is connected to his modem at. Modems can report two different speeds, but your computer can only show you one of them. The speed that you see is determined by the way your modem is set up.

Customer: Well, that's bull crap. You're just giving me the runaround!

Me: Sir, I know sometimes this can be very frustrating. But you really are connecting quite well. You simply don't understand how all this telecommunications stuff works.

Customer: Don't tell me I don't know how this stuff works, I'm an engineer for GTE.

Me (thinking 'Oh, my God'):   Well, sir, if you are not happy with the service, I'll be more than glad to refund you your money.

Customer: I don't want my money back, I want you to make this work!

Me: Our equipment is running fine. There's nothing more I can do for you.

Customer: Well, that's bull crap. You guys probably have something configured wrong!

Me: Sir, I configured everything myself; I know it's working properly. If it were not configured right, it wouldn't work at all.

Customer: You must be pretty stupid then.

Me: Look, I've had it with you. I explained to you what the deal is and you can't accept it. I'm not paid to kiss your ass! What's your name so I can have your money refunded?

Customer: I don't want my money back, and I'm not giving you my name. I AM paying you to kiss my ass, so get off of YOUR ass and fix the problem!

▶

Me: You know something, I can find out who you are from the caller ID logs, and trace that back to your account. When I find out who you are, I'll make sure that you do NOT get a refund at all, and your account will be closed anyway! Have a good day! <CLICK>

John concludes: 'I did find out who it was, and I did close his account. I never heard about the guy again; I don't know if he called my boss and got a refund or not. I don't care, but this story really sticks in my mind.'

It's certain that John did not give the customer a glow – but was it even possible? After all, the customer was in the wrong. He would not listen to reason. He was beyond reason. But we come back to the fact that dealing with customers is no different to dealing with any other human beings. As a starting point – and it's not a trivial one as we will revisit later (see page 82) – if a customer service worker can genuinely like people, everything else becomes so much easier. You can overlook their foibles. You can understand their irrationalities. We are all prepared to do this for friends and family – the same process can be applied to customers.

A good starting point is to see the situation through the customer's eyes. Mentally take yourself out of your familiar position into that of the customer. Think through what he or she is experiencing. Take what the customers say to you without applying your own values. This doesn't mean you have to be a pushover. You won't want to give in to every customer demand. Realistically, some of them are trying it on – but don't go into a discussion assuming they are. Front line staff have to be able to say 'no' to a customer – but without the chains

❝If a customer service worker can genuinely like people, everything else becomes so much easier.❞

❝Front line staff have to be able to say 'no' to a customer – but without the chains of rules and procedures.❞

of rules and procedures. It should be a reasoned judgement on their part. They will get it wrong sometimes – but it is worth accepting this price for the overall improvement in customer service.

When dealing with difficult customers more than any other we can see clearly how much the glow is reflective. We all like people who like us. We can't help it. It's flattering. Unless we've got enormous egos and expect devotion as a right, we tend to feel that anyone liking us is doing something special, and find it hard not to return that favour. There is no point in reciting that 'the customer is always right' – John's customer was wrong, there is no doubt about that. But it's much easier to cope with people who are wrong if we like them.

A fundamental component of going the extra light year, and particularly going the extra light year with difficult customers, comes down to this matter of liking. You can't force your staff to like everyone. But you can bring them slowly up to speed on the personal benefits of liking. That they will enjoy their job more. That the business will do better. That it isn't all that difficult when you get the hang of it. Most of all this is something else they will learn by example. What messages do customer contact staff get about how senior management feel about them? Do they think that the senior management likes them? Or are there barriers and distinctions? Liking starts at home.

GIVING PEOPLE WHAT THEY WANT

It seems such an obvious statement, that I didn't have this section in the chapter for a long time, yet as I collected horror stories from customers it became more and more obvious – a real obstacle to giving the glow is a lack of determination to give people what they want. Here are a couple of small examples to make the point.

❝Liking starts at home.❞

❝A real obstacle to giving the glow is a lack of determination to give people what they want.❞

ANY COLOUR SO LONG AS IT'S BLACK

'We recently took one of our five-year-old daughters into a Frankie and Benny's restaurant, a popular Italian-American chain. She was disappointed that the restaurant had run out of the usual giveaways that are part of the children's meal. Even so, she enjoyed her food, and particularly looked forward to the dessert. This was an ice-cream, topped with marshmallows or candy or something else. She wanted marshmallows and candy. "I'm sorry," said the waitress, "I can only let you have one selection."

'Apart from the bizarre penny-pinching – surely we could have had half and half candy and marshmallows? – the most remarkable thing was that the restaurant had already let us down by not delivering the full children's product, and the waitress wasn't even capable of providing this small extension of the menu to give us what we wanted.'

There's an element here of the trust component that will resurface in detail in the next chapter. It seems likely that the restaurant chain didn't trust its waitresses to vary the menu – an essential if the customer is going to get what they want.

In each case the customer was not making an unreasonable demand. They were just asking for what they wanted. And the company's representative in each case said it wasn't possible. In effect, it's saying that policy (or the staff member's understanding of policy) is more important than the customer and what the customer wants. This is a no-brainer. It would have cost Frankie and Benny's nothing to be flexible about their menu, but it seems it wasn't possible. It would actually have made Orange money to make the mobile phone swap possible, as otherwise they were going to lose a customer. And we've all known stores that won't sell you a product 'because we've only got the one in the display case, and we're not allowed to sell that'. If your policies and procedures are getting in the way of giving the customer what they want it's time to upgrade them. Or even better, like US retailer Nordstrom, to scrap them

HORROR STORY

ANY COLOUR, SO LONG AS IT'S NOT ORANGE

'I bought a cute Toshiba Portege 3110CT [laptop computer] before Xmas and want to have mobile connectivity. I find the only pain is all the ports are on the detached I/O bar, which I don't want to take round with me. It has an infra-red port, *but* I need the compatible mobile phone, for instance a Motorola L7089. Fine, my Nokia is 18 months old anyway.

'I speak to Orange about upgrading and am told I'd have to lose the 12 months remaining on my pre-paid PlanAhead contract (throwing away £80 in the process) and go back to the standard Talk30 at around £17.50 per month (I had got the same plan for £6.66 with PlanAhead) plus the £100 for the new handset (luckily my Nokia is over 18 months old or there'd be an upgrade fee too).

'So in all that would cost me £210 + £100 + £80 = £390!!!! Why the hell can't I at least have my £80 credited to the new contract? You can't – "It's company policy," I'm told.

'But, I protested, if I can find a Motorola phone from another source I can just swop the Sim [identity chip] from my Nokia and continue with the present contract – you won't know. Correct she said, but Orange won't sell me just the phone, even at an undiscounted price, so I'm forced to look elsewhere or be charged over the odds. Or I can find a cheaper monthly deal with another company (Virgin Mobile sell the Motorola at £220 and then only £12.50 connection including £10 of free calls. No monthly fee and you're billed for calls as you make them). Again it's a matter of swapping Sims to keep my number and phone book, and at the end of my Orange contract I will ditch them and move to the other supplier.'

altogether. Nordstrom's single policy is, 'Use your good judgement in all situations. There will be no additional rules.' The ultimate model.

Here is a particularly subtle example of giving the customer what they want.

GOOD NEWS STORY

PLAYING AWAY

'The experience that really sticks out in my mind is with the stereo mail-order company Crutchfield. I ordered a car CD player from them and installed it in my wife's car. Unfortunately, it wasn't accepting the CDs – it just kept ejecting them. This was a Sunday and I tried their tech support – and it was open. Again, unfortunately, the person couldn't help me because it looked like a defect in the CD player itself.

'The best part – they just shipped me another CD player without me having to send the other one back first. Therefore, I didn't have to wait for them to receive the problem one and then ship another one out. So, in a couple of days, I received the new one, installed it – and it worked. Then I sent the broken one back – of course all at their expense.'

What the customer wanted was a working CD player as soon as possible. The approach taken by most mail-order companies is first to make sure the customer isn't lying (get the original product back), *then* send out the replacement. This places a delay into the loop, so the customer doesn't get what they want. The approach taken by Crutchfield is a subtle but very effective way of building

> ❝If your policies and procedures are getting in the way of giving the customer what they want it's time to upgrade them. Or even better, like US retailer Nordstrom, to scrap them altogether.❞

charisma – giving the customer what they want when the desire hasn't been explicitly stated.

Contrast this with the problems Microsoft has had with file compatibility in its Office software. A number of times now, when Microsoft has advanced from version to version, the word processor or spreadsheet files from the new version have not been readable by earlier versions. According to a Microsoft insider, when customers complained, the developers threw their hands up into the air. 'But no one said to us "don't change the file format",' they moaned. Their customers might equally have replied, 'And no one said make the disks usable on a PC, or make sure you can read the text on the screen, but we thought this was fairly obvious.'

It should indeed have been obvious to Microsoft that this was what the customers wanted. Any large company can't cut over to new software overnight. In fact it can take years, during which different file formats can create havoc for internal communications. Okay, the customers hadn't actually specified the requirement, but Microsoft could have won plenty of brownie points by spotting what the customers wanted, even though they hadn't actually mentioned it.

It's a matter of inference and questioning. When a customer requests something, are you sure you know what they *really* want? For a long time, electrical goods in the UK were supplied without plugs. It's as if the industry was constantly saying, 'But you never said you wanted a plug on it, so we didn't give you one.' Make reasonable assumptions. If a customer wants an electrical product, believe me, they want a plug. If the customer wants an insurance policy, they want it to pay up when an event it covers occurs. (Too obvious? Read the small print of most insurance policies.) If you can't safely infer, ask.

❝Make reasonable assumptions.❞

❝If you can't safely infer, ask.❞

VALUE FOR MONEY

The more talk there is about going out of your way to make the customers happy, the more the accountants begin to twitch. This sounds expensive – but it doesn't have to be that way. You can give the glow to your customers and still make the

GOOD NEWS STORY

COVINGHAM FISH BAR

Going the extra light year isn't just the province of mega-corporations. The nearest fast food outlet to the village where I live is a fish and chip shop. It's in a small group of shops in a fairly run-down area. Yet it's special because of the approach of the people who work there. Three examples from one year:

- I had to wait a while as the fish weren't ready. The server put a piece of paper on the counter and dropped a generous portion of chips [fries] on it. 'There you are,' she said, 'there's something to eat while you wait.'

- I went into the shop and was choosing a meal. The server said: 'Did you come in a couple of weeks ago with your father?' I nodded. 'We overcharged you,' she said. 'We'll knock two pounds off your bill this time.'

- The server was putting a fish out for me and it broke into two pieces. 'That one's broken,' she said, 'I'll get you another.' And she did – as well as the fish that had broken.

Contrast the last example with the apparently good service you get in typical chain fast food outlets. Certainly they'll correct an order they got wrong – but they'll throw away the misconstructed burger (or whatever). How much more friendly it would seem, without any extra cost, to offer the fixed burger as well, not just as a replacement.

66 The more talk there is about going out of your way to make the customers happy, the more the accountants begin to twitch. 99

process value for money. As we've seen, it is still quite possible to say 'no' when it's appropriate – but we shouldn't always assume that the customer is in the wrong. The front line staff need to have the flexibility and the authority to spend money to improve customer service, provided it is done sensibly and reasonably.

Look at the chip shop examples from the viewpoint of a neurotic accountant. Each action cost the company money. These people were suicidal. But taking a more reasonable viewpoint, these actions were value for money. The free fries hardly cost the company anything, and didn't make any difference to my order. The overcharging incident was simple legality – surely the accountant isn't recommending we break the law? And the broken fish would otherwise have been thrown away. Each action was cheap, but the combination builds up to a real feeling of loyalty in the customer. I like the people, I like the place, I am going to continue giving them business.

Going the extra light year will apply more of the staff's time to giving customer service – but isn't that what they are there for? The big lesson of giving the glow is that customer service can't be left to bean counters – it's about people, not cash.

❝I like people, I like the place, I am going to continue giving them my business.❞

❝The big lesson of giving the glow is that customer service can't be left to bean counters – it's about people, not cash.❞

2

IF IT'S BROKE, FIX IT

However good your products and services, sometimes something is going to go wrong. In such circumstances, how well you fix things can be more significant than the problem. A well-executed recovery can make the customer like you even more. It's a shame, then, that we are often so grudging about this essential process.

WHEN IT ALL GOES WRONG

The acolytes of total quality management (TQM) would have us believe that the only worthwhile business goal is zero defects. I ought to emphasize before I make my next statement that I have nothing against quality, or the quality movement; achieving a quality product is an essential part of running a good business. However, I'd like to suggest that the TQM goal is dangerous and destructive. The message it gives, probably unintentionally, is that failure is to be avoided. And that the way to make things okay is through procedures and certification. So what will people do when things do go wrong? Certainly not engage their creative best, but, rather, proceduralize the problem and forget the failure as soon as possible so they can get on with being zero defect.

66The TQM goal is dangerous and destructive. The message it gives, probably unintentionally, is that failure is to be avoided.99

The trouble is, when everything goes pear shaped you have to give the customer extra attention, not less, and to move away from procedure, not stick rigidly to it. There are three ways a customer can come out of a failure. Thinking, 'What a great company; when things went wrong they really pulled out all the stops to fix it for me,' or thinking, 'That was a disaster, I won't deal with them again,' or perhaps, worst of all, thinking, 'What a pathetic excuse for an apology. They didn't even say sorry properly. It gets me so mad.'

MAKING IT WORSE

Poor service recovery is arguably worse than none at all. We add insult to injury (sometimes literally), by compounding a service failure with a failed recovery. And yet poor recovery seems to be the norm. It's not enough that we often don't apologize, or that our Byzantine procedures for determining the right compensation result in a pathetic token rather than a reasonable response, we often compound the problem by implying that the customer is at fault.

Remember the cleaning firm we met earlier (see page 16)? They will pay compensation if you first pay for an independent assessor to establish that they have damaged your clothes. What does that say? That the customers are criminals, out to rip off the poor cleaning firm, and this will remain the case unless customers prove themselves to be innocent. Yet that same company is proud that only a very small percentage of its customers have problems. So to save a very small percentage of its cash flow, it is prepared to brand all customers with problems potential criminals – and that is after they have had their clothes damaged.

The customer's feelings are critically important. Every time your customers return products saying that there is something wrong with them and you insist on checking before giving a refund or replacement, you are calling them liars (or at best, incompetent) by implication. Okay, a small percentage of customers who return things are just out to replace them with shiny new ones. A

❝Poor service recovery is arguably worse than none at all.❞

THE MODEM DISASTER

'I conduct most of my business by e-mail, so it was a major problem when a lightning strike took out my modem. I wanted to get it fixed, but to keep me going I decided to go into PC World, the local computing superstore, part of Dixon's Group retail combine. I bought a cheaper modem to keep me going, but couldn't get it working with the software that came with it. After about an hour on the phone with the manufacturer's support people, they concluded it was a hardware fault. So I took the modem straight back to the store's customer service desk and told them what the manufacturer had said.

'The response was not what I wanted to hear. They would have to check it out for me. I didn't want it checked out, I wanted my money back. The assistant was sorry, but he had to check it out. He then disappeared into the back room, which handily had large windows so I could watch what he did. His first attempt failed because the test machine he was using was already connected to another modem. He then started again from scratch. After 25 minutes he had not yet reached the point at which my problem had occurred. During this time he had come out only once, to say that it was taking quite a while. Most of the time there was no one else on the service desk.

'By now I was getting angry. Really angry. I was tempted to start playing with the till, just to get someone's attention. When the assistant came out a second time to say they were having problems with the hardware and hadn't even got to my problem I did the whole Mr Angry bit. I said that if I was kept waiting any longer I would ask for compensation for my wasted time, that I wanted a refund and I wanted it now. They gave it to me.

'It was just one error after another. They didn't listen when I said the manufacturer had identified a hardware problem. They didn't trust me, but had to check out my claim. They then proceeded to mess up the checking – and left me alone without feedback for an uncomfortably long time. The fact that I got a refund in the end was irrelevant – the damage was done.'

percentage are technically incompetent. But is it worth insulting them all, just to catch out the few?

Once again, it is common sense and reasoning on the part of the customer service agent that is going to make the difference. If a customer keeps bringing back a product because it doesn't turn on, it's worth saying something along the lines of: 'A number of people have had problems with these – they can be a bit misleading. Can you show me what you did to turn it on?' That way you can find out that he was trying to turn on a TV with the volume control without telling him that he is a fool. But many returns warrant an immediate replacement, no questions asked, with a smile and an apology.

GETTING IT RIGHT

Let's turn the disastrous recovery on its head. What is guaranteed to put a customer's back up, whatever your procedures? No apology. Yet all too often we are reluctant to take the blame. This position is not helped by the culture of litigation that seeks to punish those who fail rather than correct the fault, but often we are more worried about losing face than about litigation. We don't like to be in the wrong – so we don't apologize.

I was fascinated recently when watching a consumer rights TV show (essential viewing if you are interested in the good and the bad of customer service) to see a representative of a motoring organization blatantly avoiding the need to apologize. The topic was vehicle examinations, a service that involves

> 66 Once again, it is common sense and reasoning on the part of the customer service agent that is going to make the difference. 99

> 66 Many returns warrant an immediate replacement, no question asked, with a smile and an apology. 99

> 66 The culture of litigation seeks to punish those who fail rather than correct the fault. 99

checking out a vehicle before purchase to see if there's anything wrong with it. Out of four vehicles, each with 18 major faults, his organization had failed to spot 25 problems. What's more, the report provided gave no guidance on whether or not to buy the vehicles in question.

There was no sign of apology; if anything his attitude was truculent. He disputed the findings of the show's expert. The presenter raised one problem – a loose steering wheel, surely dangerous? No, there was a little play, but the car was safe to drive. The presenter went on to point out that people paid for these examinations to decide whether or not to buy a vehicle, but they were given no guidance. The motoring organization representative wasn't fazed. It wasn't his company's job to give guidance. They gave their customers the facts – it was up to the customers to make up their minds.

So what he was saying was, we don't give customers what they want, and we are right and won't listen to your opinions (and certainly won't apologize). It wasn't what consumers want to hear. An immediate thought on my part as a viewer was I would never use their service. The fact is that they hadn't delivered what was required and had made mistakes. Being unable to admit this only made things much worse. What do you expect from a friend when things go wrong? A sympathetic response. That's what a customer wants from a company too. Not arrogance. Not defensiveness. Sympathy and a real apology.

Sometimes an apology is enough in its own right. Despite the greed culture that the media are so enthusiastic to portray, not everyone is out for every penny they can get in all circumstances. If a friend lets you down, you expect an apology, but on many occasions, that's enough. It would seem over the top if they offered to pay you compensation, or gave you a present to say 'sorry'. The more the customers feel you and your staff are their friends, the less likely it is that compensation will be necessary. So how do you set the procedures by which the front line staff decide when to give compensation? You don't. You make sure they have the sense to make a wise decision based on circumstances.

66Sometimes an apology is enough in its own right.99

GOOD NEWS STORY

HAMPER RECOVERY

'I was recently fortunate enough to receive a food hamper from a cousin of mine. Arrangements were made to deliver the hamper during the day on the Saturday before Christmas. Saturday came and went, no hamper arrived. The following week I contacted my cousin's PA who in turn spoke to the MD of the company from whom the hamper had originated: Kevin Gould from Real Foods. Kevin was dismayed that the courier had not delivered the hamper and undertook to have the hamper redelivered.

'Eventually, by Christmas Eve we were in receipt of the hamper, which by this time was in a sorry state. Several items of food were smashed, smearing mustard grains over chocolate, with extra virgin olive oil or honey over almost everything. I contacted Kevin immediately and he arranged for an additional hamper to be sent at a time convenient for me, not the courier. The replacement was lovely, with fresh dates to die for among the goodies, all carefully parcelled and signed, "With love from Kevin".

'It was obvious that the damage had been a result of poor handling from the couriers, but Kevin's response to the news was tremendous. I will certainly be telling everybody I know how impressed I was with Real Foods, *and* what a mess the courier made of the beautiful hamper in the first place. Kevin obviously cares about his business, and his attitude will ensure that his business will go far.'

All too often at the moment, compensation is applied using a rigid, grudging system. A classic example is the approach to lost baggage taken by airlines. Because there is an international convention limiting airline liability when bags get lost, many of them hide behind these 'rules'. There is nothing to prevent them going beyond the convention – it's just there to protect the airlines. Due

66 **All too often at the moment, compensation is applied using a rigid, grudging system. A classic example is the approach to lost baggage by airlines.** 99

to this approach, all too often lost baggage is a problem that isn't effectively recovered. There might be specific hurdles to be jumped over before a customer is provided with an emergency overnight kit (you have to be travelling internationally, or at least three nights). Your compensation for a lost bag might take no cognisance of its contents. And the response might take months to come through.

Result? A disgruntled passenger. If the agent on the ground could put himself or herself in the passenger's place, in a strange location without any clothes or even a toothbrush, it would be a no-brain decision to provide an overnight kit. If the timing bore any relation to the way the airline expected customers to pay, it might have been dealt with in days or weeks. And most of all, a huge opportunity is missed by giving insulting levels of compensation. Usually the amount provided wouldn't even pay for the bag, let alone any contents. Setting a more meaningful level (realistically, in at least three figures for most bags and contents) would make a huge difference. But to set the seal, airlines should take advantage of their cheapest attractive assets – seats on planes – and throw in a free flight to a vacation destination. The opportunity is there, but it's wasted every day.

Remember, the lifetime value of a single customer to a company might be ten, 20, even 30 or 40 times his or her spend in one year. It's not unreasonable, if things have gone wrong, to pay up to a sizeable proportion of that customer's annual spend to put things right. The keys to success are trust and information.

Okay, the company might have gone over the top, but those bagels made a big impact. Compare my own experience when I opened a can of Heinz beans and found there were no beans inside, only tomato sauce. I wrote, slightly tongue-in-cheek, to complain. In response I got a voucher – to buy a single tin of beans. If you are going to get service recovery right, you can't be penny-pinching. A bare minimum with low-value goods like these should be to double the value to the customer. And vouchers are no substitute for the real thing. A

> **It's not unreasonable, if things have gone wrong, to pay up a sizeable proportion of that customer's annual spend to put things right.**

GOOD NEWS STORY

BAGELS BY THE BOXLOAD

'A couple of years ago, I was in the supermarket, when I came across an offer. If I bought a tub of Philadelphia cheese, I got a free pack of bagels. I decided to try the offer. After I returned home, I opened the pack of bagels and to say they were overcooked would be an understatement. I wrote to the manufacturer to complain.

'A week later I received a box crammed with packets of bagels, six packs of bagels, six bagels to a pack, every variety that they produce. I was most impressed by this, especially as the original pack had been free. I now had a problem, of course, because my freezer was full of bagels. As we are always quick to write off about poor customer service, I thought it only right that I should write to praise good customer service, and thus I wrote to the company to say how impressed I was and that they were an example to other companies.

'This was a big mistake, however, for a few days later an even bigger box turned up, crammed full of more bagels. Our freezer plus that of a friend is still full of bagels. Although mightily impressed by their customer service, we dare not write to congratulate them again!'

voucher means the customer has to go back to the store and buy another one (with a fiddly bit of paper that you have to remember to take, and that makes you feel like you are a charity case). Even if it ups the mailing costs, send replacement goods.

66If you are going to get customer service right, you can't be penny-pinching.99

66Even if it ups the mailing costs, send replacement goods.99

TRUSTING THE STAFF

Trust begins with the front line staff. For years, Tom Peters and other business gurus have been banging on about the importance of giving front line staff the ability to get things done themselves. But with a few notable exceptions, we fail to do anything about it. Why? Because we don't trust them enough to... er... trust them. It's frightening, really. The implication is that we are hiring either people who are out to rip us off, or incompetents. Maybe we ought to sack the people who do the recruiting. There will be a few people out to break the system. There will be a few incompetents, but mostly you will have employed good people, out to do a good job. So why do you try so hard to stop them from doing it?

All the evidence shows that moving to a situation of trust does not result in anarchy and sudden dip of profits – quite the reverse, in fact. Take the example of Nordstrom, with its single 'use your good judgement in all situations' rule. Take the example of Semco, where everything seemed stacked against trust. This was a highly unionized, blue-collar company in Brazil, a high-inflation country. It had a tradition of conflict between bosses and workers. Yet such is the trust now in Semco that many workers set their own salaries. Staff decide how much they will be paid in expenses if they have to make a business trip. Trust has achieved amazing things. And where an individual does spoil the situation by abusing it, his or her peers take it on themselves to sort the problem out – because they feel their own trust is being abused too. (See page 213 for details of *Maverick!*, Ricardo Semler's book on Semco.)

There is an implied criticism of the front line staff in the normal, proceduralized environment. 'We don't trust you to get it right. We know what should be done, but you don't, so follow these rules.' At best this will achieve automata, incapable of achieving a satisfactory service recovery. At worst it

66Maybe we ought to sack the people who do the recruiting.99

66There is an implied criticism of the front line staff in the normal, proceduralized environment.99

GOOD NEWS STORY

MOSTLY ARMLESS

'L.L. Bean, the legendary catalog house in Freeport, Maine, is known for its no-questions-asked customer service, but I put it to the test.

'I recently purchased a jacket with removable sleeves so that it could be turned into a vest on warm days. Shortly after I purchased the jacket, I removed the sleeves and promptly lost them. It was no design fault, just using the jacket the way it was intended. But I wrote to Bean's noting that the sleeves had fallen out of a special pocket in the back of the jacket designed to hold them. I observed only that in future a velcro closure might be added to keep the sleeves from slipping out as they did with me. At their expense, though I hadn't asked for a replacement, they sent me a new jacket. They even paid the cost of returning the first jacket to them.'

engenders a sense of, 'If that's how they feel about me, I'll screw them for all I can get.'

If front line staff have the ability and the authority to get things done, there is no reason to assume they will go mad with the company's money. Everything they spend comes out of their profit sharing. (What do you mean, you don't have profit sharing?) Over-the-top expenditure could put their job at risk. But getting it right can have entirely the reverse effect. If the front line representative of the company – the human face of the company – can hire me a cab to get me somewhere on time when they've delayed me, or can replace a malfunctioning product without questioning me, or can give a bunch of flowers and an apology – all without asking permission from a chain of command – I know that I'm valued. I like that person; I like that company.

TRUSTING THE CUSTOMER

Implied in the replaced product, in the compensation for the failed cleaning, is another element of trust. Trust for the customer. If it seems I'm hammering this point, it's because it is so important. The more you trust the customer, the more they will be worthy of that trust. The more you say to the customer, 'You are a criminal' the more they will prove you right. This applies particularly strongly at the point a customer makes a complaint.

The message from Ford? We are right, and you are wrong. The parts cost the customer about 1/400 of the cost of the vehicle – but Ford was happy to risk losing future custom to avoid paying the trivial amount the sun visors would have cost them. It just doesn't make sense.

Trust really can work. At the time of writing there was a battle going on between supermarkets in the UK. The two biggest chains, Tesco and Sainsbury, were head-to-head, fighting over costs. Next in line, Asda, was bought by Wal-Mart and started to expand aggressively. Yet in their concentration on costs they have ignored (as yet) a customer service first from a smaller chain, Safeway. Why? Because it involves trust. In many stores, Safeway customers can check their own goods with a scanner on the trolley as they travel around the store. This 'Shop and Go' system means that, most of the time, instead of queuing at a checkout they can present the scanner and pay. Once in a while there's a random check, but speaking to customers, this isn't

**❝The more you trust the customer,
the more they will be worthy of that trust.❞**

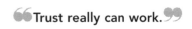

HORROR STORY

CROSSING THE FORD

Here's an example of Ford getting it horribly wrong.

'I've always bought Fords – my Dad did too. A couple of years ago I spent more than I've ever spent before on an automobile. A Ford MPV – seven seats, superb flexibility, great to drive. I love it. After about a year both flaps fall off the mirrors on the sun visors. They replace them, and Ford pays part of the cost. After less than a year, both the new flaps have broken off. The mechanic tells me there was a design fault, and they're now made differently, but because the car is two years old, they won't pay. I write to Ford to complain.

'Three months later, I get a letter from Ford, asking for more information. I give it to them, pointing out the delay. Soon after I get another letter. It apologizes for the original delay – I like that – but wait for it. It says "We are always willing to consider financial assistance outside the Ford warranty. However, we hope you will understand that we have to take account of the age of the vehicle and the nature of the repair. Inevitably, many parts sustain wear and deterioration during the lifetime of the vehicle and there must come a point where we can no longer offer any help. We are sorry we are unable to provide any assistance on this occasion."

'What they took no notice of was both the mechanic's claim there was a design fault and also that we weren't talking about original parts. These were less than a year old. And as for wear and tear, I never use the mirror on the driver's side. That flap had been lifted maybe two times before it fell off. Customer service? Don't make me laugh.'

seen as a negative thing – in fact it's as likely to find them overpaying as under. The big supermarkets are battling on cost, the weapon of the loser – if one of them picked up on as big a customer service point as this (because, let's face it, the worst part of supermarket shopping is going through the checkout) things might be very different.

GOOD NEWS STORY

MAGNETIC SUCCESS

'Everyone expects trouble when they buy a kitchen. Everyone has a horror story about their experiences of getting the wrong things delivered, things falling apart, and so on. I was no exception. As per usual things went wrong. I was rebuilding an entire house and the builders fell about a month behind schedule – no problem. Magnet, the kitchen vendor, stored the kitchen and told me not to worry about it, they would deliver it when I needed it.

'Then came delivery day and we had a few units delivered incorrectly and a wrong worktop and a number of other details that weren't right. But what made Magnet so good is that they were very quick to respond (correcting the mistakes within 24 hours) and made the whole thing a much more stress-free process than usual. I know the order should have been right in the first place, but usually it is much easier to impress a customer when you quickly and cheerfully rectify a mistake than if everything was fine in the first place.'

This talk of trusting the customer is all very fine, but it all falls apart when it comes to security. Most retail outlets feel the need to have elaborate security precautions to foil shoplifters. These are often expensive in manpower and equipment, so there must be good evidence that shoplifting would otherwise be a serious problem. The trouble is, many anti-shoplifting measures brand everyone a criminal. A more creative approach would be to find measures that only impacted the criminal (or distracted them from ever committing the crime), something that can be seen at some bank counters.

Compare the counters of a railway station and these banks. In the UK, at least, railways put their attendants behind a glass screen with a small grill to speak through. Any transaction has to be made via a well under the grill, or a

> **66 This talk of trusting the customer is all very fine, but it all falls apart when it comes to security. 99**

rotating turntable. In the more advanced banks, such as the Halifax, despite the more serious risk of robbery than at the station, things are very different. There is no grill or glass screen. You are face to face with the teller, who can hold a real conversation with you, unlike the hunched, uncomfortable transaction at the railway station. But it doesn't mean that the bank has forgotten security. Unlike the railway companies, the bank assumes most customers aren't criminals – so they can interact normally. But high-speed shutters will cut a criminal off from access to the teller. The norm is trust – but the backup can deal with those who aren't worthy of it. And that's the way it should be.

KNOWING IT ALL

It's all very well saying that we should give the front line staff more freedom and trust to get on with the job, but to give them freedom alone is to miss out an essential tool for the job. Alongside trust there has to be information. Look at that prime example of trust in action, Ricardo Semler's Semco. Yes, staff can set their own salaries – but they have the information they need to reach a sensible figure, and everyone else knows what they earn as well. Yes, they can claim whatever expenses they feel are appropriate for a business trip, but they can base it on real costs, not numbers in a manual – and once again, anyone in the company can see what they spent.

If the customer contact staff are to have the freedom to act as they see fit, they need information that will help them in their judgement – and perhaps to know that anyone else in the company can see just what they did do. We'll venture more into information about the customer in a later chapter ('They know me'), but think for a moment about the airline customer who has lost her bags.

66It's all very well saying that we should give the front line staff more freedom and trust to get on with the job, but to give them freedom alone is to miss out an essential tool for the job.**99**

While the customer service agent can make a fair guess at what the passenger means to the company, it will remain a guess. She could be a millionaire and regular flier who likes to dress down. She could be an obviously wealthy person who has no intention of flying with your airline again – either because she hates flying or she has her own private jet. She could be a business commuter who clocks up thousands of miles a week. But there's only so much the agent can deduce. How much better if the agent can be given some guidance. To know that this is a regular passenger, or a heavy spender. Perhaps even to have some estimate of lifetime value. Of course there's an element of guesswork here. But the more relevant information you can give, untainted by unnecessary garbage, the better chance the agent has of making a wise decision.

THE POSITIVE ERROR

Every now and then the problem can actually be in the customer's favour. You send them too much money. You deliver too many goods. You undercharge for your services. If the customer notices the mistake and is honest enough to tell you about it, you are being handed an opportunity for displaying charisma on a plate. Don't waste it.

GOOD NEWS STORY

NO WHINING

'We buy wine by mail order from Bordeaux Direct; during the summer our order of two cases arrived twice. Being basically honest, I rang and told them; they located the error, apologized, and said that they'd send a van to take it away, unless we'd like to buy the second lot at 30% discount. It was probably cheaper for them than arranging carriage to return it, but the way it was done left me feeling good about them.'

66 The more relevant information you can give, untainted by unnecessary garbage, the better chance the agent has of making a wise decision. 99

The mail-order wine company won the customer over with a very small gesture. I would have been inclined to say 'Keep a bottle from each case as a thank you, and you can buy the rest at a 30% discount if you like.' When a customer has been honest like this, the more fuss you can make of them the better. There's something particularly satisfying about being honest when a fuss is made of you – it's your company's job to make sure that the fuss is significant.

Simply to take the goods back without comment is a disaster. You have turned any warm feelings the customer might have about you to ice. At the very least, they should get a thank you letter from a senior person in the company. But some form of reward is much more appropriate. After all, the customer has just saved you some money. You can afford to give them back a percentage. That way, everyone is happy, the customers bathe in the warm glow of their honesty, and appreciate your company for its generosity. I suggested giving away a couple of bottles in the wine example, because the discount, however generous, still requires an outlay on the customer's behalf. A gift is unconditional.

IT'S NOT OUR FAULT

It's quite easy to see the necessity to put things right when you've made a mistake. But what about fixing someone else's disasters? Even if it's a competitor? A natural reaction might be to stand back and laugh, but this is a situation where you can get a big leap ahead of the competition.

66When a customer has been honest, the more fuss you can make of them the better.99

66A gift is unconditional.99

GOOD NEWS STORY

EVERY TIME YOU SAY 'GOODBYE' I SAY 'HELLO'

'I had decided to change cell phone provider, not because there was anything wrong with Hutchison Telecom, who provided my phone, but because I wanted a specific handset that wasn't available on their network. I went for another, smaller company.

'The new company was terrible. It was almost as if they didn't want my business. After a couple of weeks trying, I still hadn't managed to migrate to the new system. I explained this to Jan, the contact at Hutchison who was dealing with my migration. She took everything in hand, sorting out the other operator, making sure everything went smoothly. I was very impressed.

'A year later, when my initial contract expired with the smaller company I went back to Hutchison for at least 15 phones. And it was all down to Jan.'

When things go wrong and the competitor isn't sorting it out, consider it your business to do something about it. Don't be grudging, be very, very visible – and *your* customers (because before long they will be your customers) can't fail to notice.

PRE-EMPTIVE FIXING

A final thought about putting things right. All too often we wait for the customer to complain before attempting service recovery. How much better if you can undertake a pre-emptive strike. Get in there and make things better *before* receiving a complaint.

Just imagine yourself in this position. Your train was late (again). Very late. You go home and mutter about the railway company. But two days later, in the

66When things go wrong and the competitor isn't sorting it out, consider it your business to do something about it.99

66Get in there and make things better *before* receiving a complaint.99

mail there's a box of chocolates and an apology letter from the railway. It would be totally amazing. Or again, your bank fails to pay the interest on your account one month. You haven't noticed yet, as you don't check your statements until the end of the quarter. Next month, however, you get a letter apologizing and telling you they've not only paid in both months' interest, but doubled it. Now that's service.

It's all too easy to come up with a list of excuses as to why you can't act in this pre-emptive manner. It would be too expensive. It is exposing mistakes that some customers haven't even noticed. It would be very difficult to track the customers anyway. But that doesn't mean it's not worth trying. The railway company, for instance, might not know everyone who was on a particular train, but they do know who had reservations for it. The bank has no technical obstacles, only a philosophical one. But remember what is happening here. It might seem you are fixing what is not broken, but in fact there are plenty of irritated customers out there. Not irritated enough to write and tell you, but certainly irritated enough to take their custom elsewhere. Beware this silent majority. Mostly they complain with their feet.

ORANGE PROBLEMS SQUASHED

To end this chapter, a final example of good recovery. On page 40, a customer of the Orange phone network described her frustration at the charges she would have to face to change her handset to one that would work with her new PC. After I got in touch with Orange to get their side of the story they came back to the customer and not only did what she wanted, but threw in the phone – all for free. Orange generally has a good customer service record, and this excellent (if under media pressure) recovery is more typical of their approach.

66 Beware this silent majority. Mostly they complaint with their feet. 99

3

I'M IN LOVE WITH MY CAR

Sometimes charisma is generated by the product. This can be a fantastic asset that many large companies squander without consideration. It is often seen in the case of vehicles (though they are by no means unique), in the love affair we have with cars of character and great motorbikes.

SOMETHING SPECIAL

In an almost mystical way, a product or brand can have a quality that customers love. Such products develop a near-fanatical following. One component of winning over the customer is cherishing products or brands with a magnetic attraction. Many such products have reached this state unintentionally in the past, but there is now a clear enough picture of the elements that make up a classic product that it is possible to steer in that direction. You can't guarantee the outcome. Some attempts at producing a classic have been total flops. But you can certainly influence the chances of making it, and be sure once a product achieves classic status that you treasure it.

Be a little careful, however. Having a well-loved product certainly ensures a loyal customer base, but it carries a price. Those customers will feel that the

66 Some attempts at producing a classic have been total flops. But you can influence the chances of making it. 99

product is theirs and may turn against you if you take an action that seems detrimental to the product or its survival. This will obviously happen if you discontinue the product, but even lesser changes of direction can result in a bumpy reception. For instance, when Apple, whose Macintosh computer is definitely in this category, announced a joint venture with Microsoft, seen by many Apple fans as the great enemy, Apple representatives were jeered at and booed.

I DON'T LOVE MY...

It can be equally instructive to look at the products that have bombed. What was it about a particular item or brand that ensured that no one would love it? We presume that the designers didn't set out to produce a product to hate, or at best feel indifferent about – but it is often the outcome. A whole class of products – basic 'me-too' items – fall into this category. So do most household goods and everyday products. But do they have to?

As we examine the categories of loveable product, spare a few moments to think of everyday objects, and whether it's possible to give something ordinary enough of the special characteristics of a loveable product to make it special. Think also of your products. What would it take to give them something extra in this particular dimension? We'll start with what's probably the strangest of them all – being quirky. Sometimes, bizarrely, it's almost as if there being something wrong with a product can make it attractive.

QUIRKY SUCCESS

Quirkiness is a strange characteristic. A quirky product may be slightly difficult to use. It might be rather ugly. It may break every design rule in the book. But there is something endearing about its otherwise off-putting nature. Quirkiness

> 66 Having a well-loved product certainly ensures a loyal customer base, but it carries a price. 99

> 66 Sometimes, bizarrely, it's almost as if there being something wrong with a product can make it attractive. 99

is best explored by example. All the examples we look at may have other loveable characteristics, but they are also quirky.

On the road, there are certain cars that have generated a love affair. Citroën's 'upside down pram', the 2CV. Fiat's tiny cars. The British Mini. They have so much more character than the me-too, streamlined boxes that most of us drive. Such quirky cars are rarely high performance. In fact, they are often downright slow. But they're simple to repair yourself (the 2CV famously was designed to be serviced by the village blacksmith). They're distinctive. And they're fun. Often they don't work quite the same way as everyone else's car. 2CVs had windows that opened outwards like fanlights, a gearshift that was a strange knob disappearing into the dash and seats that pulled out for picnics.

2CVS

'I enjoy the simplicity of a 2CV, the ease of doing anything to it. It has timeless design. You can get parts anywhere and perhaps I have an affinity with the type of people who choose to own one.'

When you drive a quirky car and see another one on the road, you wave and flash your lights. You are part of a club that needs no membership details and no organization – the very ownership of the car makes *you* special too. When a member of our family owned a 2CV, for quite a while one of the windows was tied up with a piece of string to stop it flapping open. Somehow this seemed to typify all that was wonderful about the car. This quirkiness seems to stretch to most vehicles over 30 years old. The sheer fact of owning and preserving a car or a wagon that predates air conditioning and stereo (not to mention heating, windscreen wipers and speedometers in some cases), gives the vehicle that edge.

In the UK, cars that have gained this quirky appeal have included the original Volkswagen Beetle, the Citroën 2CV, the Morris 1000, the Mini and Morgan's unique line of timeless sports cars. At first sight they've not that much in common. They're mostly cheap – but the Morgan isn't. They're foreign, except when they aren't. But they're all different from the crowd, they are all quirky and fun – they all have charisma.

HORROR STORY

THE RENAULT ERROR

Renault's innovative run-around the Twingo has proved very popular in France and elsewhere, but Renault has not produced a right-hand drive version, so it has never reached the UK. This is a real case of a company shooting itself in the foot. The Twingo has everything going for it as a car to fall in love with. Renault claim that it's a technical problem that has stopped them from bringing the Twingo to right-hand drive countries – it's a technical problem that should have been overcome, as it could have transformed Renault's image.

It's not all about cars, though. As we've already seen, the Apple Mac brought a revolution of quirkiness to personal computers. Ever since 1984, when the Mac ads burst on the screen during the Super Bowl it has been obvious that there was something very different about these machines. The message of the ad was that the Mac was the computer for the rest of us, smashing the Big Brother grey unity of the (by implication) IBM world.

Everything about the original Mac said quirkiness. Its very origins in a remote building flying a skull and crossbones flag made this inevitable. All those features we take for granted now – the graphics display, the mouse, the icons and the windows – made it so different. The strange, upright casing with its built-in screen. The sealed box you couldn't get inside to see the signatures of its designers impressed in the plastic. Even its early trademark habit of crashing with a bomb symbol on screen – Macs weren't just tools, they were objects to love.

❝The Apple Mac brought a revolution of quirkiness to personal computers.❞

All sorts of other products have the same feel. Many are generic – it's the way they are, the way they act that make them quirkily attractive. Analogue synthesizers. Hand-powered coffee grinders. Hand-tied bow ties. Calculators that use reverse Polish operations. Slide rules. I have a circular slide rule that was my father's, a wonderful instrument with a shining chrome casing and smooth-turning knobs to rotate the scales on what would be a six-foot rule if it were linear. It's pathetic when compared with a calculator, but I love it. Quirkiness counts.

CLASSIC DESIGN

Some products transcend their nature and function. They might be as mundane as a kettle. As everyday as a chair. Yet there is something about the product that makes it stand out so far above its peers that it becomes loveable. Such classic design is often about simplicity. Classic chairs might have the simple, sexy curves of an Italian marvel, or the Spartan lines of Shaker furniture or the designs of Charles Rennie Mackintosh. They may well not be the most comfortable chairs, or the most flexible. But the simplicity and naturalness is breathtaking.

As I walk around the house I am impressed time and again by the impact of a few classic items. There is something special about using them every time. A Maglite flashlight, practically anything from the Swedish geniuses Ikea, French screw-off beer bottle caps – even something as everyday as the paperclip when designed well.

Two specific household items that I love: Philips' Onis phones. These cordless digital phones just feel right in the hand. They're balanced to sit

❝Quirkiness counts.❞

❝Some products transcend their nature and function.❞

❝As I walk around the house I am impressed time and again by the impact of a few classic items. There is something special about using them every time.❞

comfortably, they work superbly, and they slip back into the cradle with effortless smoothness. Even as small a design element as the holes in the receiver to let the sound out have been made to look interesting. Then there is Bosch's US-style fridge-freezer. Most fridges in the UK are small and cramped. This huge double-doored fridge-freezer with its ice maker and smooth drawers makes the apparently boring business of storing food fun.

Back on the road, the definitive example of classic design has to be the UK's Morgan Cars. This small company's current models were launched in 2000 and the 1960s, but both maintain the spirit of 1930s' design, and each car is still hand-built on a wooden frame. The customers love it – as witness the several years that you have to wait to buy one. It was interesting that when industrialist Sir John Harvey Jones gave Morgan the once-over in a TV show called 'The Troubleshooter', while he was shocked by the old-fashioned and inefficient ways in which the cars were built and suggested radical changes (some of which have gradually been taken on board), he didn't suggest any change to the product itself.

One company that seems to have underestimated the power of classic design is Coca-Cola. Not only did it do so over its recipe in the famous debacle when New Coke was rejected in favour of the classic flavour, it has mostly scrapped its own iconic design masterpiece, the traditional Coke bottle. With one of the two most distinctive soft drink bottles in the world, it is crazy that Coke, usually a master manipulator of marketing, hasn't brought back the old curvy bottle in a big way. The other distinctive bottle? France's Orangina, luckily still in every supermarket in France, despite the threat from plastic bottles and cans. And long may it remain.

We are often so obsessed with designing for novelty that we miss the power of a classic. Every rule in the book says that Morgan couldn't possibly still sell cars with a 1930s' design – but the reality is quite different. The only catch is you've got to have great design. Not the everyday outpourings of designers who

❝One company that seems to have underestimated the power of classic design is Coca-Cola.❞

don't understand people, but just want to show off their own cleverness. Classic design is usually simple and joyous. It sets off a natural resonance that all the smartness of fashion can never equal. By all means keep up with the crowd, but if you ever get your hands on a classic, guard it with your life.

PRODUCTS AND BRANDS

Though Coca-Cola may have disregarded an iconic design element in the old Coke bottle, the very product has this special charisma. To most of the world it says something about the American way of life. Quite how a soft drink can be endowed with such properties is something of a mystery, but Coke has got it, and it has got it big. However much Pepsi has tried to challenge Coca-Cola, it hasn't broken through. There was a time when Pepsi used to focus on taste tests, proving that in a blind tasting customers preferred Pepsi. They entirely missed the point. You don't drink Coke for the taste, it's for the cultural experience.

To a lesser extent, this same aspect of imbuing a product or brand with the ability to generate a unique feeling is present elsewhere. A number of airlines have tried, with varying success. Singapore Airlines made a big thing of the 'Singapore girl' (when it was still politically acceptable to do so), but passengers found the reality didn't live up to the promise. More impressively, when British Airways was at its customer service height in the late 1980s and early 1990s, it generated a special feel all of its own. Customers spoke of feeling that they had come home when they got onboard a BA plane from a very foreign country. Interestingly, it wasn't just UK passengers who reported this.

66By all means keep up with the crowd, but if you ever get your hands on a classic, guard it with your life.99

66Coke has got it, and it has got it big.99

COKE IS A CONSTANT

In a century of dynamic change – technology, science, family structure, the waning of religion – it was only Coke that stayed the same, offering membership to a universal club. It has permeated the lives of people to such an extent, it has become associated with almost every aspect of consumers' lives – first dates, being at college with friends, moments of success – all the 'feel good' moments in people's lives that Coke knows how to play on and build images on.

People have assimilated the imagery that has gone with the company from the start, some 109 years ago. The company has invested heavily in promotional tools and advertising to such an extent, that nearly everyone on the planet is aware of the product. It has become an intrinsic part of everyday life. The raison d'être of Coke is to be the number one seller in every market they enter, and the gearing towards this is promotion. In 1990, Ike Herbert, Coca-Cola's head of advertising said, 'We are who we are because we are all things, to all people, all of the time, everywhere.'

This is true when you realize that Coke has an exclusive presence at over 400 prestige US locations such as Disney World, Madison Square Gardens and the Yankee Stadium, and as such, is encountered by over 280 million patrons a year. Coca-Cola has been able to create such extensive brand awareness and brand loyalty due to its ability to conduct one activity with great success – to identify the commonalities of human experience. Coke patterns its advertising to appeal to virtually all human beings. Coupled with its global presence, Coke is available to everyone, and means something to most of them.

From a thesis by Gregor D. Cosgrove

66 Customers spoke of feeling that they had come home when they got onboard a BA plane from a very foreign country. 99

THE SEEDS OF LOVE

All these products and brands have something in common. They generate emotion in us – they have charisma. It is the ability to influence our feelings that is at work. This implies a lack of blandness, yet also an ability to ignore fashion and do your own thing. It is a high-risk strategy. Those who ignore fashion can be mocked. But hit on the right combination, the right emotional response, and the rewards can be immense. Working towards a charismatic product like this should not be a lone strategy, as it is so high risk, but ought to be a parallel task to the mainstream of any large company. And when you hit on your success, the quirky, the classic, the sheer loveable product, hold onto it for a long, long time. It will be worth it.

66 Hit on the right combination, the right emotional reponse, and the rewards can be immense. 99

4 THEY KNOW ME

There is something very special about companies who genuinely know you. What large companies have found to their cost is that while you can fake this to a degree – perhaps by using people's names – to get the real charisma factor out of this asset you have to be dealing with real people who genuinely know you – which may require a much more fragmented organization of a company.

THE SMALL COMPANY FACTOR

Any large company is fighting against a major disadvantage when compared with the small fry. Each and every customer of a small company is known, and if the company is any good, is cherished. That's a whole lot harder to do when you've 10,000 or 1,000,000 customers. There's a burgeoning market of customer relationship management (CRM) systems to try to cope with this problem and bring the small company factor into the corporate. Anything that can help manage the customer relationship better has to be good for building up charisma. But any relationship is a two-way interaction between human beings, something that shouldn't be forgotten when computer systems vendors

66 Any large company is fighting against a major disadvantage when compared with the small fry. 99

make their pitch. To understand CRM, don't start with computers, visit a village store.

Probably the biggest difference between a corporate and a small company is that the small company knows its customers personally. When Miss Smith comes into the shop and buys a packet of sweets for 20p, the shop owner knows that she spends £20 a week with him. That's a potential lifetime value of around £40,000. Take the 20p at face value and you could make a big mistake. CRM is about giving big business some of the small guy's advantage in knowing more about the customer. Because, get it wrong and in today's fickle society, she'll abandon you overnight.

What is it that the small shopkeeper can do that a large business can't? First, he can recognize Miss Smith. His customer base is small enough to know each regular shopper individually. Second, he has a broad idea of that customer's value. Not explicit numbers, but enough to know whether Miss Smith is a small spender or a high-value customer – if she's high value, he can work harder to keep her trade. Third, he knows Miss Smith's preferences. He can have her newspaper ready, or stock her favourite sweets. And finally he can make the experience more pleasant for her by having an informed conversation. He can ask about her mother's health or the holiday in St Ives. All of this adds up to giving Miss Smith satisfaction, and that increases the chance of retaining her custom.

It is difficult for a big business to give that same feeling. If you can identify an individual, a CRM system can supply as much information as possible to the company's representatives so that they can understand a customer's value and provide a personalized service. It's not the same as really being known, but it's a start. Unfortunately, you have to be able to identify the customer first. Nowhere are the advantages and challenges of CRM clearer than in e-

66Anything that can help manage the customer relationship better has to be good for building up charisma.99

66Probably the biggest difference between a corporate and a small company is that the small company knows its customers personally.99

GOOD NEWS STORY

BISTRO MEMORIES

'The best example I can think of was from a little bistro on the Isle of Wight. My wife and I had dinner there twice when we were in the area on vacation. It was excellent. So when we were nearby a year later, we just had to call again.

'We were impressed when the owner welcomed us, saying "Great to see you again," but assumed he was guessing from the booking. But what really took us aback was when we were seated. "The same table as last time," he said. "But I see this time you're facing the other way." My wife and I had swapped places – he was right. It was incredible. We recommended this place to everyone we met for years after until the owners moved on to a different enterprise.'

commerce. At first sight it may seem that the e-commerce merchant is crippled by distance. How do you have a relationship with an invisible customer? Yet e-commerce has a real advantage over conventional business. The ability to identify the customer.

Compare the small shopkeeper, a major high street store and an e-commerce merchant. When Miss Smith comes through the door, the shopkeeper instantly recognizes her. The high street store can't. While the customers browse, while they make their selections, while the purchases are added up at the till, the shop assistant won't know who this person is. The only chance comes at the end of the transaction when the customer pays, and only then if they don't use cash. The e-commerce merchant is almost as fortunate as the small shopkeeper. Web

66Nowhere are the advantages and challenges of CRM clearer than in e-commerce.99

66E-commerce has a real advantage over conventional business. The ability to identify the customer.99

sites can store small files on a customer's PC. Provided the customer accepts these 'cookies' (most do), the e-vendor can use them to recognize the customer on future visits and kick in a CRM system.

THE DANGERS OF CRM

But even if you have managed to recognize a customer, don't think that having a good CRM in place is the answer to all your problems. In the end, relationship management is a people issue, not a systems issue. At best, the system can supply the right people with the right information at the right time so that they can simulate the sort of relationship that the small business really has with its customers. I'm not knocking this, but if you rely on the system to do it all you will get nowhere.

Although it's easy enough to get wrong, the systems side is the easy part. It's still the personal relationship between your front line staff and the customer that is going to make all the difference. A CRM should always be regarded as second-best – it would be much better if you can find a way to handle the customer exactly as a small company does, by really knowing him or her – and the siren song of the systems salesperson needs to be examined very carefully. Yes, your relationship with your customers is crucial, but don't assume that buying a system is going to make everything wonderful overnight.

DOING THE BASICS

It's amazing how much can be done without any system in place. When you walk into our local village shop, the shopkeeper says 'Hi!' with a big smile. The sort of welcome you give to someone you know. It's very different from the sort

66In the end, relationship management is a people issue, not a system issue.99

66Yes, your relationship with customers is crucial, but don't assume that buying a system is going to make everything wonderful overnight.99

of reception you get practically anywhere else. Yet he doesn't need to know the customer to do it. I've seen him do it to perfect strangers – and there's no problem. They appreciate the friendliness, while the regular customer interprets it as a welcome recognition. If you are a regular customer of a large company, you usually get to know a few faces among the staff. If they gave you this sort of welcome, you would feel the recognition was mutual, an instant bonus for the company's attractiveness.

It's still the case, for that matter, that more often than not when I use a credit card, the attendant doesn't take the opportunity to use my name. It doesn't matter how much it happens, I still get a little thrill when someone says, 'Thank you, Mr Clegg,' or whatever. No system, no magic. Just a little thought on the part of the server.

GOOD NEWS STORY

WINE WAITING

'I was doing some work in Australia and I stayed at a large hotel in Sydney for a couple of weeks. A week later I was back there again and there was a bottle of red wine waiting for me in my room with a message from the manager saying that he was pleased to see me back and he believed that this was the wine I'd enjoyed when I'd stayed before.

'When I tracked him down (he was off duty for a couple of days after I'd checked in) and asked him how he'd managed this he admitted that it was pure chance. He'd seen my name in the forward bookings file, checked the credit card used to guarantee the booking and found I was the same person. It was then easy to find one of the wines I'd had when I'd eaten in the restaurant. What impressed me most wasn't that he was able to do this but that he'd bothered. I spent the next few years saying to anyone who was going to Sydney that they had to stay at this hotel (unfortunately I've forgotten the name now).'

66No system, no magic. Just a little thought on the part of the server.99

While we're at it, let's go back to those regular customers of a large company. Chances are, someone in the company knows them. I regularly take my children to the local supermarket on Saturday morning. We reward ourselves by having breakfast in the supermarket restaurant. One day I was alone, and the server on the till commented that this was unusual. It made me feel special – she knew me. Okay, you can't do it for every customer, but there are few customer contact staff who don't have a collection of well-known customers they recognize, however large the company. When my wife worked on the counter of a branch of one of the UK's largest banks, she knew and could chat with practically every regular customer. Customers would bring her presents at Christmas. One even asked her to go on holiday with him. You don't always need a system.

IN CONVERSATION

Basic conversational skills should be among the prime decision factors in employing customer contact staff. Yet going on the many cheerless souls I have to deal with as a customer, it seems not to be high on many employers' lists. Just having a basic stock of conversational throw-away lines – we aren't talking major dialogues here, just a simple comment on the weather or a topic of interest in current affairs, or simply, 'That's a nice jacket' – would be enough to transform a conversation with a front line staff member from a chore to an enjoyable experience.

With the benefits of a CRM system it is possible to go further. If the system pops up appropriate information about that customer there is an opportunity to make use of it. But there is also an opportunity to misuse it. A good parallel is

66There are few customer contact staff who don't have a collection of well-known customers they recognize, however large the company.99

66If the system pops up appropriate information about that customer there is an opportunity to make use of it. But there is also an opportunity to misuse it.99

the way I find caller ID works in the home. Our home phones flash up the incoming number before we answer. If it's someone in our address book they show the name. It's actually quite rare that we pick up the phone and say, 'Hello, Carol' (or whatever), both because it's a little unnerving to the person on the other end, and it loses impact if it happens to be Carol's husband instead. However, what the caller ID does allow us to do is to get in the right frame of mind for the type of call it will be, take a quick preliminary action or even (very occasionally) switch on the answerphone.

Similarly, it doesn't do anyone any good if practically the first thing you say to a customer is, 'Ah, good morning, Mr Smith. I see you bought from us five times already this year, and your last invoice was for twice as much as usual.' Chances are Mr Smith is feeling by now as if Big Brother is breathing down his neck, and somehow even feels guilty that last time he spent twice as much as usual. Just to make sure, he will spend half as much this time – not exactly what you were trying to achieve.

Instead, the information should bolster the conversation, bringing it into areas that might be of mutual benefit. Pointing out, for instance, that to order slightly more this time would take his annual total into the next band, resulting in considerable savings in the future. A lot has been made in relationship management circles of using CRM systems to give the impression that the staff member really knows the customer. This can be done by saying, 'Oh, hello, Mr Smith. Nice to have you dealing with us again. You booked three people on courses last time – do you want to do the same again?'

That's fine if you are sure that the staff member in question has dealt with Mr Smith before. If not, it might be better to make it clear what is happening ('I'll just check on the system… ah, yes, it was…'). In fact even with a staff member who has handled Mr Smith before it might be worth making the statement into a question. Few people's memories are good enough to be definitive. If, for instance you decided to throw in a social comment, it would be

❝A lot has been made in relationship management circles of using CRM systems to give the impression that the staff member really knows the customer.❞

better to say, 'Weren't you moving house last time I spoke to you?' with a natural degree of uncertainty rather than the creepily sure, 'You were moving house last time I spoke to you.'

BEING INTERESTED

In looking at the basics, I pointed out how a simple smile and 'hi, there!' with the right tone could imply that the customer was known. The easiest way to ensure that your customer contact staff are effective at this approach – and at making comfortable conversation – is to ensure that they are interested in people. It seems an oversimplification, but that single quality, being interested in people, may be all you need to differentiate between good customer contact staff and great customer contact staff.

Everyone makes a decision about the rest of the world. You can regard other people as fascinating or boring. You can take the elitist view. That the majority of people (people who aren't *us*) are a faceless crowd with little individuality. That their little lives are of no interest. That they are moronic cash cows to be milked for all they're worth. Or you can see them for what they are. True individuals with their own ways of doing things, their own hopes and dreams. Real people with real experiences. That this is a practical view is demonstrated by the huge popularity of fly-on-the-wall documentaries on the TV. These docusoaps have proliferated, partly because they're cheap to make, but also because people are interested in people. So why do they switch this interest off when they go to work?

It starts with an attitude. The same attitude that says, 'If it wasn't for the customers, this job would be great.' That's an attitude that has to be stamped out remorselessly. If it wasn't for the customers there would be no job. No money. And plenty of boredom. Customers may sometimes cause difficulties

❝It seems an oversimplification, but that single quality, being interested in people, may be all you need to differentiate between good customer contact staff and great customer contact staff.❞

❝Everyone makes a decision about the rest of the world.❞

(although often it's your systems that cause the difficulty and all the customer is doing is reacting), but most customer contact staff would rather have a steady stream of customers than a whole day without speaking to someone.

So the customer contact staff have to be encouraged into docusoap mode. Not to see the interaction with the customer as an irritating interruption, or a meeting with a brainless idiot that is wasting the staff member's time, but an opportunity to have a fascinating glance into someone else's life. Voyeuristic? Maybe, but we're all voyeurs at heart. How much better to find someone else interesting than to find them boring. The choice is down to the staff member.

Many organizations find particular difficulties here with young staff. At risk of being ageist, young people have real problems in service roles. First, secondary education has taught many of them that having an interest in things – an interest in *anything* – is sad and boring. This is an entirely unnatural state for the human animal to be in, but our schools achieve it through peer pressure (and occasionally through bad teaching).

Second, even if they have an interest at their own level, many young people think that older people are inherently boring – after all, they're not young and never were.

Dealing with these difficulties is not trivial, but it is important. One option is not to employ young customer contact staff. Companies that employ older workers in customer contact jobs from call centres to DIY superstores regularly report that a better customer relationship develops. The customers trust the staff, the staff members respect the customers. But that isn't always an option, and while it is ludicrous that companies often exclude the valuable over-fifties from employment opportunities it is equally sad if young people aren't given a chance to grow in a job.

“Most customer contact staff would rather have a steady stream of customers than a whole day without speaking to someone.”

“While it is ludicrous that companies often exclude the valuable over-fifties from employment opportunities it is equally sad if young people aren't given a chance to grow in a job.”

Where younger staff – under 25 or so – are taken on, there should be conscious efforts made to help them with an interest in people. This may be helped by broadening their interests in general – perhaps using sponsored activities to expand their interest beyond bars and discos. But there also needs to be conscious education in the personal benefits of becoming interested in people, if only to make their own day more enjoyable.

LIKING THE CUSTOMER

One step beyond showing an interest in the customers is liking them. It's a big step in terms of results, but quite a small one in practice. While it's possible to be genuinely interested in something you don't like (spiders or a mass murderer, say), it is usually the case that an interest brings liking in its wake. It's hard not to like someone you are interested in. And it's hard to give bad customer service to someone you like. If it's possible to take that step from interest to liking, the charisma component will be firmly in place. From the customers' viewpoint, once they think about your company, 'They like me!' there can be no going back. It's almost impossible to be liked without returning the compliment.

The fascinating thing is, just as interest in the customer makes the job less boring than before, liking the customer again hikes up the benefits for the staff member. Once you like your customers, the concept of a difficult customer becomes much less common. What you've got is not someone being difficult, but someone you like who has got into difficulties (quite possibly because of your horrendous systems) – and helping them out is going to be like doing a favour for a friend.

It's not that Natasha Keal didn't have her share of those who would traditionally be labelled difficult customers, but she chose not to see them in that way because she liked them – she liked people, period. She saw something good

66 **If it's possible to take that step from interest to liking, the charisma component will be firmly in place.** 99

66 **It's almost impossible to be liked without returning the compliment.** 99

NO MORE DIFFICULT CUSTOMERS

Consultant David Freemantle gives a superb example of how difficult customers can disappear in his book, *What Customers Like About You* (see page 211 for details).

'Two years ago I was running a seminar in the USA and the debate inevitably got around, once again, to how to handle difficult customers. A number of participants related some vivid anecdotes about problems that they had faced with customers. Suddenly, one young woman, Natasha Keal, put up her hand and waited patiently to be invited to speak.

'"I find this very strange," she said quietly, "but I can't recall the last time I had a difficult customer. All my customers are very nice to me and I never have a problem with them."

'Natasha smiled as she spoke. She had a soft, warm voice with a trace of an Irish accent. I invited her to explain why this could be so. Why was it that all her colleagues in other branches seemed to have problems while she did not?

'"I just treat my customers like friends," she explained, "all of them. If I get a mother coming in stressed out with a screaming baby in a buggy, I do my best to help. If I get an old lady coming in grumbling about our charges, then I listen to her, explain as best I can and try to be nice to her. If I get some bum coming in drunk then I'll crack a joke, process the transaction quickly and guide him quietly out the door before he annoys the other customers."'

in everyone. This sounds like Pollyanna stuff that might have many of us reaching for a sick bag, but it's not. Natasha's approach doesn't require you to pretend everyone is wonderful or a saint when they aren't. Just to accept that they're human beings with something good in them, even if it isn't showing right now, and that by recognizing this, everyone will benefit – the customer, the staff member and the company. It's such a shame that most of us choose the less pleasant, less rewarding experience, because it is a choice.

Liking the customer comes across as being a friend, rather than someone who is just out to get your hands on their money. And one point we all like to have friends to turn to is under pressure, when we need reassurance. This can be a great time to show off your corporate charisma to the customer.

GOOD NEWS STORY

BANKING ON CUSTOMER SERVICE

'Last year my partner and I were buying a house, and I was trying to sell my flat. My buyer pulled out at the last minute, so I was in the position of having to find an £18,000 bridging loan within a few days to secure our purchase. I phoned my bank – Lloyds TSB – on the off chance that they might be able to help, and was amazed at the service I got. They took a few details over the phone and invited me in to see the manager the next day.

'When I arrived he had already worked out the combination of overdraft and loan that I needed, filled in all the paperwork and got the necessary approval. He recommended that I swap my normal current account for a "gold service" current account, which gave me a discounted interest rate on the loan. He also explained how I could avoid paying more interest than I needed to, which seemed odd for a bank! The loan was paid into my account the same day.

'Lloyds TSB didn't even make much profit from the loan as I paid it off within three weeks (which they didn't penalize me for), but they definitely gained my goodwill (and another gold service customer). I was so impressed with their service – which was both professional and incredibly reassuring at a time of extreme stress – that I have a great sense of loyalty, which must be extremely unusual for customers of the average retail bank. This is a good example of an organization that treats potentially profitable customers well, in order to keep their business and in the long term, make more money out of them!'

66This can be a great time to show off your corporate charisma to the customer.99

DOING IT ONLINE

It might seem at first sight that the online world of the Internet is not a practical place to give the warm glow of recognition to the customer. Certainly there's no question of having as much impact as a real human interaction can have on the customer's emotional state. But the online world does have the advantage of being able to store a customer's details triggered by a small file on the customer's computer called a cookie.

With a cookie to identify the customer you only have to ask for details once – after that you know who they are. This means you can greet them. When I enter the online bookshop Amazon, it says, 'Welcome back Brian Clegg'. Not exactly conversation, but at least it's friendly. You can also make things easier. Sticking with Amazon, when I find a book that I'm interested in, there's a button labelled '1-Click™'. If I press that button, I buy the book. I don't have to do anything else – give a credit card or a delivery address – the system knows who I am. It makes buying from the e-shop less hassle than conventional shopping.

1-Click is only the start. An e-commerce CRM can track the customer throughout the site. It can monitor every page visited, every button clicked. From this knowledge it is possible to customize the customer's view. Bill Wittenberg of Art Technology Group, a company specializing in Web customer relationship management, points out that an essential reason for personalization is speed. Unless you make it easy for customers, they won't stay. A CRM behind a Web site can mean that your second visit reflects the interests of your first. If you looked at classical music in a music store, now classical music is more prominent on the front page. This sort of approach is particularly important for

❝The online world does have the advantage of being able to store a customer's details triggered by a small file on the customer's computer called a cookie.❞

❝An essential reason for personalization is speed. Unless you make it easy for customers, they won't stay.❞

a broad-based site that is attempting to match the focus of a much smaller site – the Web site equivalent of the comparison of the corporate and the village shopkeeper.

With enough information you can also make judgements based on the customer's value. You can give special offers and discounts, or open up whole new sections of your catalogue to a high-value customer. And the knowledge that drives this decision should not be based solely on information from the Web contact. A good CRM should be able to pull together all a customer's interactions with your company, whether it's over the Internet, the phone, in person or by post. This works both ways. If someone shows a lot of interest in laptops on your Web site, this can influence your conventional mail shots. If possible, such integration should continue into the broader business information systems to provide a complete overall picture.

MAKING IT REAL

If the aim all along has been to bring the small company feel to the customer relationship, and hence not only to make the customers feel that you know them, but to *actually* know them, there is one final step that can be taken. Make it come true. Don't fake it, do it. Go back to the village shop's advantages by making your business into a collection of village shops.

In *DisOrganization* (see page 212), a book written with Paul Birch, I suggested that one of the best directions for organizational change was to split into a series of mini-companies, each effectively a small company in its own right and typically between around one and 50 people in size (see Figure 1). The mini-companies would be coordinated by a central net company that kept information flowing and brought the mini-companies together in a general direction, whether they were part of the same structural organization or totally independent.

❝A good CRM should be able to pull together all a customer's interactions with your company.❞

❝Don't fake it, do it.❞
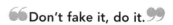

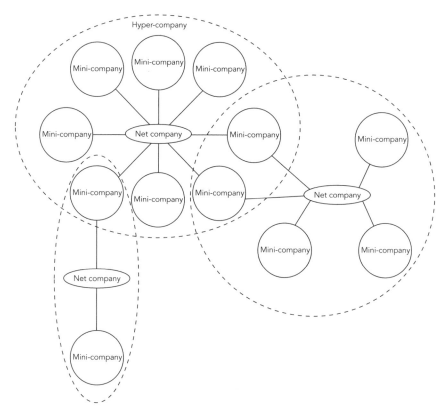

Figure 1   The mini-company and organizational change

This isn't the place to go into all the details of a mini-company approach, but from the viewpoint of charisma it has a lot going for it. Mini-companies are small enough so that everyone in the company knows each other. As with any other small company, there is a much better chance of contact staff in a mini-company knowing customers than in a faceless conglomerate. If your aim is to get small company benefits into a large company (and there are many), there

❝If your aim is to get small company benefits into a large company, there can be no more effective way than actually developing small companies within the large.❞

can be no more effective way than actually developing small companies within the large.

Even if this isn't achieved, however, it is possible to go part of the way. Most of us like the fact that we have *a* GP or *a* dentist, despite the fact we're only one customer of a huge medical industry. It's someone we know and trust. They know us. Okay, occasionally we have to deal with someone else, but generally we get all those advantages of being known as an individual. There's no reason why most companies can't take the same approach of having a principle contact person for each customer. They won't always deal with you, but they can most of the time – and that way both the company and the customer will get most of the benefit.

5 STAR POWER

It's easy for grey people in grey suits to criticize the apparently self-seeking approach of company superstars like Richard Branson. However, there is a real transfer of affection to our stars. We are interested in them; we like to associate with them. Too little attention is paid to the stellar potential of senior executives and front people.

SELF-PROMOTING IDIOTS?

If you work for a competitor of one of Richard Branson's companies, the chances are you don't take him too seriously. Maybe that should be qualified. As a businessman, yes. As a dangerous competitor, yes. As an expert at finding the edge – definitely. But then come his antics in the media and the corporate eyebrows go up. Whether he's ballooning around the world, queuing for rides at a theme park or featuring in a documentary, Richard Branson is a performer through and through. I still remember a TV show in the early days of his airline, where he was shown entertaining passengers by performing tricks (like 'stealing' a watch).

To the average board member, such behaviour is simply not appropriate for the top management of a serious company. There's often a feeling that being in business should not be about fun. It's a serious business that should be treated

❝There's often a feeling that being in business should not be about fun.❞

appropriately. So Branson's publicity-seeking stunts are dismissed as trivial. They are considered to reduce his status. But in this belief, the average board member is sadly mistaken.

The fact is, however much you may dislike it (could there be an element of jealousy here sometimes?), having a household name heading up the company makes a difference. A big difference. Ask anyone in the street for the name of the chairman or chief executive of most big-name corporates and you'll draw a blank. Ask them what they think about the company, and you will get an equally blank response. It's seen as a grey organization with dull people doing dull things. Ask them about Virgin and you'll hear something different. They know who Branson is. They identify Virgin with a youthful, lively, innovative approach. It's something many customers want to be associated with – and it is Richard Branson's star power that is largely responsible for this.

WHAT IS A STAR?

As long as there have been mass communications, there have been stars. People whose name and face are recognized by the public. People who get pointed at as they walk down the street. People the public are interested in and want to know more about. They might be from the movies or music, from sports or TV. They may be known for what they do that's special – or just for being good at being known (the magic word there is usually 'celebrity'). It doesn't really matter *why* they are famous, once someone is a star, people are interested.

You have to be a little careful here. Some stars are as highly segmented in their appeal as are some brands. They might be incredibly famous in one country and almost unheard of in another. They could appeal just to the youth market or only to the over-sixties. This isn't necessarily a drawback if you have a focussed product or service – but it has to be borne in mind.

66 **Having a household name heading up the company makes a difference.** 99

66 **As long as there have been mass communications, there have been stars.** 99

Whatever the market segmentation, however, a star is a desirable commodity. A star will attract media attention like a charisma magnet. Some publications, such as *Hello!* magazine, are dedicated simply to what stars do, but even mainstream media and serious news shows are more likely to cover an issue if a star is involved. From the media's viewpoint, stars sell copies, or advertising, or ratings. Once upon a time a star was a glamorous performer, or someone who had conquered an extreme like climbing Everest or reaching the poles. Nowadays, a good definition of a star is someone who can capture media attention without doing anything in particular.

TAPPING THE AURA

The traditional approach to benefiting from a star's media exposure is endorsement. Especially in the USA, it is absolutely the norm to have a star extolling the benefits of your products on TV and in the magazines, even if there is no possible connection between the star's claim to fame and your product or company. You might have a golf player advertising a flatulence tablet or a rock star enthusing over a lawnmower. It doesn't seem to matter as long as the name is there.

A superb example of this is Michael Jordan, the Chicago Bulls basketball player. In the late 1990s Jordan became the apotheosis of star as brand. In the first nine years of the decade he made over $300 million from his assorted salaries and endorsements. In just one year, his endorsements topped $45 million. Jordan's star quality took him far beyond endorsing and advertising sports goods. He is also an excellent example of the way a star can combine being immensely powerful and parochial in influence. In Europe, where basketball has much less of a following, Jordan is practically unknown.

66 **Whatever the market segmentation, a star is a desirable commodity.** 99

66 **A good definition of a star is someone who can capture media attention without doing anything in particular.** 99

This regional variation can also apply to the reaction to endorsement itself. One of the big differences between US and UK cultures is that UK audiences are much more cynical. While you will still find some use of this approach – the 'scientific' popular broadcaster Carol Vorderman advertising a margarine that claims to reduce your cholesterol levels, even though her qualifications are in maths – it tends to be used more subtly. A star will appear in an ad almost incidentally. Their presence will endorse the product, rather than their fulsome praise. Otherwise, UK audiences assume that the person in question will say anything for money, and the result is to degrade the star's image, rather than improve the image of the product.

Endorsement is not the right vehicle for attaching charisma to a product or company. While there will be a small influence from the UK-style presence on advertising, most customers are well aware that stars appear in adverts because they are paid to do so, not because they have any connection with the company. Instead, really to influence the customers, the stars have to be directly connected to the product, brand or company... or at least to give that impression.

Making such a strong tie between a company and an individual can pay huge rewards, but there are risks as well. If the individual suffers bad publicity, so can the company. In the UK some years ago, Ratners, one of the largest chains of jewellers was totally wiped out as a brand. The reason? Gerald Ratner, very much the front man of the company, made the mistake of mocking his own customers when making a speech. What he had intended as a witty, throw-away remark to a select audience got huge media coverage. Customers left Ratners in droves. In fact, whenever the person at the top gets in the media, star or not, they need to be very careful what they say.

❝One of the big differences between US and UK cultures is that UK audiences are much more cynical.❞

❝Making such a strong tie between a company and an individual can pay huge rewards, but there are risks as well.❞

HORROR STORY

IT'S A JUNGLE OUT THERE

The Web shopping company, jungle.com, had some problems with customer service in 1999. The founder of the company seemed determined to sort things out. He appeared on a TV show, proclaiming how important customer service was to the company. And he sent out a personal message to his customers. Part of it read:

'As the founder of jungle.com, I would like to personally apologise to you, if you are one of our valued customers who have experienced a delay in receiving your order.'

One of their customers was impressed with this obvious intention to put things right personally and replied to the man at the top as follows:

'The week before last I decided to purchase a palmtop computer, and having decided on a Palm 3x, decided to order from Jungle. I wanted next day delivery. On the order page there are three buttons, one of which you have to click on in order to get next day delivery. It wasn't obvious that this was what was needed, and so I continued on, and was surprised to find that I'd actually ordered. On any other Web site that I have ever made a purchase, there has always been a page that lists your order so that you can check the details before confirming the order.

'Having placed an order I didn't want, I then phoned to ask that the order be amended for next day delivery. It turned out that this wasn't possible, and the order would have to be cancelled, and I would have to place another order. I did so. This time I clicked on the relevant button to indicate next day. I completed the transaction, but as there is no screen to indicate what you have ordered, I didn't know if I'd done the right thing. It is very frustrating to have to go into the order checking section to confirm the details of an order you have just placed.

'On checking the order online I found that it did not indicate next day delivery. I phoned again, and once again had to cancel the order. I was told that once I clicked on the next day delivery button, I then had to click on another button on the page to update that page. That is crazy, when again, any other site I've been to just understands which button you've clicked on, and carries the information over.

'I placed the order again, this time succeeding in making it next day delivery. This was for delivery on Saturday. On Saturday afternoon I called Jungle to ask why it hadn't arrived. I was told that you were out of stock, and that it would arrive the following Wednesday. I was very annoyed that I hadn't been called, as you did have my phone number. Having placed a next day order, I had stayed in especially not to miss the delivery. I cancelled the order.

'I subsequently received a phone call letting me know that my order had been cancelled. I assumed this applied to all three.

'Today, on Monday over a week later, I have taken delivery of a Palm 3x. I don't want it. I believe that under consumer law I am obliged to give you six months' leeway to pick it up, after which I own it. Please arrange for collection at a time convenient to me.

'I have tried calling the customer care number, but it rings without an answer.'

Eleven days later, with no response at all from jungle.com, the customer tried again, using the customer service e-mail address.

'Having received a message from your founder, I would have expected that he would have replied to my response. There is little point in apologising for bad service if you just make it worse.

'I have tried calling the customer care line a number of times, but it's more like a customer don't care line, without even a message to say you're in a queue.

'You sent me something I'd cancelled. I will be disputing the charge with the credit card company. The order number is 654744. I'll be in next Saturday morning if you want to arrange to pick it up.'

Over a month later, still no response. He tried again and finally received a call. This generated the following e-mail.

'Having not heard from you for weeks, I sent another e-mail on Wednesday. You left me a message on my mobile on Thursday to say that you were picking up the goods on Friday from my home, at any time between 9 and 5.

1   I was unable to retrieve my voicemail until late on Thursday.

2   The lady who left the message did not leave a phone number that I could call.

▶

3　The lady who left the message told me the address to which to address the parcel. She spoke quickly and unclearly, and I don't know if the address I have is accurate.

4　I left the parcel with a neighbour on Friday. The neighbour was out for about an hour total during the day. I don't know if anyone arrived to pick up the parcel, because the parcel was not collected, and there was no note through the door to say that anyone had been.

There's no point in arranging a pickup without making sure someone will be in. My mobile number is…'

The story ended more by accident than intention. Jungle.com finally rang to arrange to pick up the goods on a Friday. No one came. As it happened, the customer was in when the courier arrived on the following Monday. He said they knew nothing about a Friday pickup. Subsequent apologies? None.

In this story there was administrative chaos, but the key factor was the way that the man at the top laid himself on the line – and then proceeded to ignore a real customer who responded to his message.

SOMEONE UP-FRONT

The simplest way to achieve transfer of charisma from the star to the company is to have the star head up the company, or at least come somewhere close to that, with a fuzzy enough involvement that they can be said to own or run the company. In some cases this is literally true – there's no question of Richard Branson's involvement (though some of the Virgin companies have been spun

66The simplest way to achieve transfer of charisma from the star to the company is to have the star head up the company.99

off) – in others there's an element of fiction – the group of stars who front Planet Hollywood have little involvement in running the company, but the effect is the same.

Bearing in mind that stars can be made or brought in, stardom at the top has emerged from both directions. A small sample of famous names to have companies or brands built around them include Paul Newman (salad dressings), the late Linda McCartney (vegetarian foods), Bruce Willis *et al.* (Planet Hollywood). As well as Branson, others to have been pushed to the fore purely as a result of their business include Anita Roddick (Body Shop), Victor Khyam (Remington), Jan Carlzon (SAS) and Bill Gates (Microsoft).

Sometimes the association can be very specifically with a product. This is often seen in leisure software for computers. You might have a garden design product with a TV gardener's name on it, or a sports simulation that apparently 'belongs' to a superstar. The process goes even further with books, where novels and autobiographies, apparently written by a star are in fact written for them for a fee.

But whether your front person is actually involved with the running of the business or just window dressing, the important thing is that they have media penetration, and use that penetration to get the message across. With a star involved, the launch of a new product or service is much more likely to get media coverage – and whatever your advertising agency tells you, editorial coverage has overwhelmingly greater impact than advertising when it comes to charisma. With a star at the helm, it is possible to highlight all those particularly charismatic elements of a company that you can't really advertise. The environmental and charity work that you do. The way you give your customers and staff a good time. Your uniqueness.

MAKING STARS

Stars don't have to be born – they can be constructed. It happens all the time in show business. Some actors may be stars because their ability is head and

66With a star involved, the launch of a new product or service is much more likely to get media coverage.**99**

shoulders above the rest, but many of them are there because the Hollywood publicity vehicle has put them there. It has happened in the music business too. When in the 1960s the group the Monkees was constructed by a TV company to be rival to the Beatles there was nothing new about a process that the recording industry had undertaken for years. And it still goes on – most recently with the group S-Club Seven.

To some extent the same process can be applied to people at the top of your company. You need the right sort of people, of course. Not every chief executive is a budding star. But with an appropriate approach to public appearances and a popular response from an audience, there's no reason why your top people couldn't become stars for your benefit. Look at how others have achieved this:

- *Through advertising.* Putting the person at the top in the ads can be effective, but beware the klutz effect. If the result is amateurish, there is a possibility you will still win across an audience who find the performance cute or entertaining, but there is equally a possibility of alienation.

- *Through personal interest.* Developing a strong interest in an extreme activity – whether it's ballooning around the world, climbing mountains or walking to the poles has a good chance of getting attention. Beware the stuffed dummy opportunities, though. If your chief executive is into movies and you sponsor an awards ceremony, don't let him or her give out an award – they will just look impossibly awkward alongside all those professional performers.

- *By being there.* If your business tends to be in the press regularly, you can increase visibility by making sure that your would-be star is always at the forefront of press events. This approach is particularly handy if your company features in a docusoap. Don't just have the key person cutting the ribbon or making a speech – make sure they do something entertaining like juggling, wearing silly clothes or otherwise making a spectacle of themselves, thereby proving that they are good sports.

66Stars don't have to be born – they can be constructed.99

- *By getting involved in public works.* There are usually opportunities for senior business figures to get involved in government-initiated schemes. Richard Branson, for instance, was very visibly involved in a campaign to remove litter from London. Make sure that the scheme in question is media attractive; there is little benefit in heading up a sewage treatment committee. A variant is involvement in high visibility charity events like telethons – but again, not just by providing a cheque. The would-be star needs to show that he or she has character and is prepared to get stuck in by doing something unusual.

- *By taking part* in TV game shows, chat shows, panels and other 'names wanted' activities. Avoid daytime shows unless they have a particularly strong impact on your target audience. Also make sure they give the right image – the British royal family notoriously damaged its public image when younger members took part in royal version of the farcical game show 'It's a Knockout'.

Star making doesn't generally happen overnight. It will take repeated exposure over a couple of years to make an impact. But the benefits to the company could well repay the effort.

RECRUITING STARS

If the person at the top lacks star potential, or simply considers it beneath his or her dignity to have a public persona, you can always buy in a name. As has already been stressed, this involves more than a simple endorsement or even the beauty care company's habit of making a star strongly associated with the product. The idea is to give the impression that the star either started the company, runs the company, owns the company or has a major input to the way the company is run.

There is actually a double benefit from this. If the star has some involvement, even if it only involves dropping in twice a year, the employees will get a boost

66 **Star making doesn't generally happen overnight… But the benefits to the company could well repay the effort.** 99

from their presence (assuming, of course, that the star appeals to the employees' demographic). They will feel that they are part of an organization that is a little bit starry, and this can carry through to their performance, particularly if the star makes frequent contact with front line staff. The main aim, though, is to hang onto the star's publicity aura and spread the charisma to the company.

At the very least, you can ensure that your pet star is a shareholder. However, many stars are not as one-dimensional as their PR sometimes portrays them, and may have a genuine interest in how the company works and give real input to direction. This has certainly been true of the likes of Paul Newman and the late Linda McCartney.

BEING THERE

There is a price to pay for having a star at the top of the organization. It becomes expected that the stars will be available to front any public campaign that they are needed for. That's fine with a pure figurehead who can be kept on 24-hour standby ready to wheel out on any occasion, but it's a lot harder if the star has a real job to pin down, particularly if it involves flying around the world negotiating deals for the business. It might be wonderful that Richard Branson is the face of so many Virgin publicity campaigns, but it means if he isn't available, it will seem that the particular event is considered unimportant by the company.

There was a good example of this happening in UK politics in 1999. Analysts decided that the ruling Labour Party's bad showing in the European elections was in part down to the involvement of Tony Blair in negotiations in Kosovo. Blair attempted to play the star role as premier, and paid the price when the crisis in the Balkans made his presence there essential. It was the right thing to do in world terms, but his party suffered.

66 Hang onto the star's publicity aura and spread the charisma to the company. 99

66 Many stars... may have a genuine interest in how the company works and give real input to direction. 99

A number of options are available to counter this problem. You could go for a pure figurehead, or someone more junior in the company for the star. You could make sure that the star had enough trusted representatives that there wouldn't be an occasion when he or she couldn't be pulled out of what they were doing to front up to the public. You could take the occasion to the star if the star can't come to the occasion. This consideration does not detract from the value of having a star; it just means the implications should be thought through before the first occasion when the star misses a big event crops up.

FUN AND FROLICS

Something that can hold senior executives back from taking the limelight, or from having a front person that does, is the aim to have a serious, businesslike image for the company. There is still a concern that investors, the markets and others could frown on anything less than sober, reasoned behaviour. Not only is there good evidence that this stigma no longer applies – it has hardly done Richard Branson any harm – there is a positive benefit from an attitude at the top of the company that says fun is okay.

Generally speaking, while the revenue is delivered from the bottom of the company, the culture is set from the top. If the top people put across a message that having fun is acceptable, that this isn't a stuffy place to be, that culture will percolate through to the front line staff unless you make positive efforts to stop it. This means the front line staff will enjoy their work more, and be under less stress. It also means that this sense of fun will come across to the customer. While there are occasional businesses where it may be inappropriate (funeral directors spring to mind), generally having a smiling customer contact who clearly enjoys his or her job is a real benefit in getting the customer to relate to the company. There's a double benefit here.

66 Take the occasion to the star if the star can't come to the occasion. 99

66 Generally speaking, while the revenue is delivered from the bottom of the company, the culture is set from the top. 99

ANYONE CAN BE A STAR

The prime focus of this chapter is on having a star running the company, or at least as a figurehead, but it's quite possible for the company to benefit from anyone within the company becoming a star, provided they keep their allegiance to the company. A good example would be Pat Kerr, the British Airways flight attendant who founded a children's home in Dhaka as a result of her experiences with poor children on stop-overs. As a result of two TV documentaries, she became something of a celebrity in the UK – and the positive publicity did the airline no harm.

I am not suggesting that employers should try to use such publicity as an active endorsement (and this certainly wasn't the case here), but by allowing an employee who gets this sort of media attention the freedom to do what is necessary, the employer can benefit from reflected glory. It doesn't have to be good works either, of course. You could have an employee who has a hit single or is a world-class athlete, but doesn't want to give up his or her career – fine, make use of it (and in such circumstances you can get in there to the hilt).

In one sense, of course, this section title should apply to your whole front line workforce. They all can and should be stars as far as their customers are concerned. But that's an associative extension of the meaning of 'star' – this particular component of charisma is about the real thing. In the next chapter, however, we will look at getting all your customer contact staff shining.

❝By allowing an employee who gets… media attention the freedom to do what is necessary, the employer can benefit from reflected glory.❞

❝Your whole front line workforce… can and should be stars as far as their customers are concerned.❞

6 THEY'RE PEOPLE LIKE US

In an earlier chapter we considered how an important component of charisma is getting the customers to feel that you know them. This factor has a reciprocal of similar benefit. The more your customers can identify with your staff as real people, the more they will like them and the company. Putting peoples' names on badges isn't even a start – because real people don't have their names on badges.

EMPLOYEES ARE PEOPLE

Hopefully, it doesn't come as a shock to you that your employees are people. In some companies the staff might argue that they are treated more like performing animals or components of a production line – but of course that doesn't apply to your company. That's just as well. A company with charisma is liked or even loved by its customers. The easiest way to achieve that is if the staff are liked (or even loved) by the customers. But it's hard to love an automaton, a mechanical unit in a production line that spouts a mechanical script while undertaking a set of pre-programmed actions.

The more you can get your customers to see your employees as individuals, as real people that they can (and want to) relate to, the better your chance of

It's hard to love an automaton.

developing that love affair with your company. As with the fun in the previous chapter, there's an added bonus too. The more you treat your staff as real people, the better the job they are going to do for you. The customers may not always be right, but they are certainly right about this one.

GOOD NEWS STORY

POST HASTE

'Our postman is great. When he first started on our round he noticed when we got birthday cards. The next year, he gave us each one on our birthdays. If he comes to deliver a parcel that needs signing for and he notices our bedroom curtains are shut he comes back later on his own time so he doesn't disturb us.'

I had another example of great service from a UK Royal Mail customer. In this case, the postman knew a customer was in the process of moving and made sure that the mail went to the right address, even though there was no formal redirection in place. It makes me wonder if Royal Mail know what stars they have working for them – or even would appreciate it if they did know. What's certainly true is they miss out on a huge opportunity. They have representative going to most houses every day. Why doesn't the mailman sell stamps – or many other value-added products?

SMALL COMPANIES WIN HERE TOO

Here's another place that the small company has a natural advantage over the big corporation. Not only is it easier for the small company to know its customers, it's easier for the customer to know the company – and specifically the individuals who front it up. 'Individuals' is a key word here. Big companies

66 The more you treat your staff as real people, the better the job they are going to do for you. 99

don't really like individuals. Most large companies (there are a few brave exceptions) try to squash the life out of individuality. Apart from anything else, it makes things easier. If you can regard your staff as a set of interchangeable components (and I have known company directors who have taken this view literally), you can shift them around as and when you like to suit business requirements. Of course, you'll end up disrupting people's social lives and careers, but they're just cogs in the machine, so what does it matter?

If, however, you regard your staff as individuals with different skills and talents and personal requirements, you have to work a lot harder to get the best out of your workforce. The result will be output that is streets ahead of the best the 'cogs in the machine' director achieves, but you have to be prepared not to be a lazy manager. This isn't the only reason individuality is suppressed, though. It also offends the sense of corporate neatness. Uniformity looks neat; individuality looks messy.

Put like that, it seems a trivial argument. Yet it's the basis for many of the rules and regulations with which most companies like to strew their business. Take uniforms, for instance. Everything from an army uniform, through the burger bar apron to the regulation business suit is designed to do one thing – take away individuality and replace it with sameness, and implied neatness. Often the individual will find some way to show through. Corporate suits often seem to have a secret competition to find who can wear the most eye-splitting tie or braces [suspenders]. Some companies, like the effervescent T. G. I. Friday chain, encourage their staff to customize the uniform, in this case with their own choice of hats and a plethora of badges. But the aim frequently remains to suppress individuality.

It doesn't stop with clothes. Some US companies still have an aversion to men wearing beards, a bizarre injunction given the historical precedents; these are companies that would not employ Abraham Lincoln. The suspicion has to be that it's not that they have anything against facial hair – it just smacks too

❝Big companies don't really like individuals.❞

❝Uniformity looks neat; individuality looks messy.❞
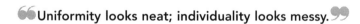

much of individuality. With customer contact staff in particular, the aim seems to be to smooth everyone down to be a plastic clone of the ideal person.

Contrast this with the small company. The chances are that as a customer you will know the individuals who work there. They will have their own distinctive clothing style and appearance. Their behaviour is their own. They have individual, distinct personality traits. Some of these you might not like – that's the risk the small company takes. That's the risk the large company eliminates. But in the process of eliminating that risk they throw out the baby with the bathwater. Because it is individual, distinct personality traits that enable us to identify, relate to and like other people.

It also helps that there are fewer people in the small company. Sheer weight of numbers in a big business makes it hard to develop a real relationship with the staff, unless each customer has a personal representative as suggested earlier. Compare, for instance, our local pub with the nearest T. G. I. Friday's. When we had gone into both around half a dozen times, we were in a totally different state of relationship. Despite the personalization of the uniform, T. G. I. Friday's staff basically look the same. Even if there was a chance of getting the same server on each visit it would be hard to pick them out. At the pub, the distinctive dress and conversational style of a server soon built an easy relationship – and within those half a dozen visits she was starting to call us by name.

Although weight of numbers poses some problems, there is no reason why large companies should not achieve that small company feel and those small company benefits in terms of making staff better known to customers, as the rest of this chapter will show.

66 With customer contact staff in particular, the aim seems to be to smooth everyone down to be a plastic clone of the ideal person. 99

66 Although weight of numbers poses some problems, there is no reason why large companies should not achieve that small company feel. 99

NAMES ON BADGES

Go into most companies with uniformed customer contact staff and you will see name badges, often bearing an uplifting message like 'here to help you' or 'have a nice day'. There is something particularly bizarre about this most uniform of attempts at individuality. Rather than encourage the building of a natural relationship, it almost ensures that you don't, presumably entirely contrary to the intention of the company. You can be as friendly as you like, but summon a waitress with whom you have had no social interaction by saying 'Jane!' having seen her name on her badge and you aren't echoing a normal conversation, but rather the patronizing master–servant relationship of the Victorian era. You aren't on an equal basis; she doesn't know your name. It's entirely unnatural.

This has not gone unnoticed. Where it's practical – for instance in a restaurant where the customer is seated by a greeter – there is usually an attempt to establish a more natural introduction. They will say, 'This is Jane, who will be looking after you today.' The theory is that you've been introduced, so you now feel that you have a relationship, however shallow. But it is still a one-way opening. It would be interesting to see the reaction if Jane responded, 'Hi, and what are your names?' and went on calling her customers by name after that. It may be done in some restaurants, but I don't have any feedback on the outcome.

The fact remains that in most environments where the customer contact staff wear name badges you are not introduced, and the usual effect on the customer is to give them the opportunity to speculate that, 'He doesn't suit the name Kevin', or, 'What's the point of having a badge that says "D. Spackman", who is going to say "Hello, D. Spackman" and I wonder what D. stands for?'

Compare this situation with my usual ideal for customer relationships, the village store. After a visit or two, as you become recognized as a new regular, you may well be asked if you've just moved in. It's a chance to say, 'Yes, I'm Brian Clegg – we bought Mrs Wilson's house on the hill,' and in the normal

66 **The theory is that you've been introduced, so you now feel that you have a relationship, however shallow.** 99

conversational way of establishing the first steps of a relationship, the shopkeeper can say, 'Oh, really? I'm Sylvia, by the way.' Or whatever. Like all normal human interactions, there isn't a standard script. There are a thousand ways to find out names and begin to use them – the important thing is that it feels natural. You might overhear another customer calling the shopkeeper by name. At some point in the future, when it feels right, you might use it. But there is no need for badges. This is real life.

Is the village store model possible in a large business? Not in every case, but surprisingly often. On the telephone it's much easier, where asking and giving a name is part of the ritual – but many businesses working this way miss out on the opportunity and don't have their customer agents pick up on the names and use them. In large stores, regular customers will often come to recognize some of the staff, especially if they stay in one department. I've occasionally given a smile of recognition to someone in the street only to realize that they work in my local supermarket, or sit on the left-most till at the bank. Again, this is usually a wasted opportunity.

Note, by the way, another example of the battle between individuality and uniformity. At one time a bank clerk would have 'their' physical till, the one they always sat at. Such individual ownership of the till made it easier to develop a relationship with an individual. When bank clerks became seen as inter-changeable components, there was much less opportunity to get the recognition. Funnily enough, the multi-queue – a single queue accessing multiple servers – also reduced the chances of building a relationship as you can't go to your 'favourite' server but go instead to the one you are directed to. Despite the advantages of such queuing systems for uniformity of waiting time, it might be worth considering dropping them if you are working on giving more personality and individuality to your servers.

Consider other ways you can make your customer contact staff more individual. Is the uniform really necessary? A uniform isn't the only way you

66There are a thousand ways to find out names and begin to use them – the important thing is that it feels natural.99

**66This is real life.99**

can look smart, after all. And if you need a uniform to identify who the employees are, there are more subtle ways of doing this that still allow for individual appearance. Are there other ways staff could personalize their working environment so that when dealing with them you know you are dealing with an individual? It might have your corporate design police spinning in their designer chairs, but some degree of personalization can also put across the message of humanity. Certainly, however you decide to do it, those name badges should go.

A FAREWELL TO SCRIPTS

How you look is part of the recipe of any relationship – what you say is another fundamental ingredient. If we are to relate to the customer contact staff we deal with as real human beings, they have to be capable of real human conversation, the antithesis of the script. Like most customer service disasters, scripts were developed with the best of intentions. The idea was to achieve consistency of service, making sure that all customers got the offers they were entitled to and were exposed to the appropriate sales pitch. Scripts can also help protect your back, so that when, after the event, the customer complains you can say, 'We warned you, it was in the script.' Unfortunately, while scripts do achieve consistency, they achieve consistent awfulness.

I suffered a good example of why scripts are always going to destroy, rather than help build relationships a while ago. I picked up the phone and cheerful voice told me how he wasn't selling anything. 'Oh, really,' I responded with the lack of enthusiasm you might expect. 'Yes,' came the reply. 'Well, you sound really full of beans,' he carried on doggedly, 'What's your secret?' I was so taken aback, I couldn't reply. I patently didn't sound full of beans. This was grossly

66It might have your corporate design police spinning in their designer chairs, but some degree of personalization can also put across the message of humanity.99

66Like most customer service disasters, scripts were developed with the best of intentions.99

artificial. There was no stopping him; you could almost hear the clockwork ticking in his brain. 'You must have had a good weekend!' In fact, I had spent most of the last two nights sitting up with a sick child. 'No,' was my short reply – just before I hung up.

Even an innocuous burger bar script can lead to the uncomfortable clash of brain cells against robotic precision. If you try to cram all the elements requested by the script into your order, the server will often overload and continue as if you haven't spoken, so that the conversation goes something like: 'Two super-quarter-pounder meals, please, with Coke, to go. I don't want any extra ketchup or anything.' The server nods. 'What drink do you want with the meals?' You sigh. 'Coke, please.' Another nod. 'Eat in or to go?' Fine. 'To go.' A minute later he has everything packed up. 'Do you want any extra ketchup or salt?' Rather than commit justifiable homicide, you say, 'No thanks,' and leave with an over-wide fixed grin.

Scripts have more than one problem. Not only do they not suit every customer and every situation, they don't suit all the front line staff. Given the opportunity, each individual would have a different style, a personal way of operating that would distinguish him or her. Not only would this make it easier for customers to identify specific staff members, you would also find that different customers had different server styles they preferred. Some might want the quickest possible service, with no frills. Others might want more of a chat. Some might like the ready informality of youth, others the greater care of an older server. Disposing of scripts doesn't just give the customer an interaction with a human being. As they get to know different front line staff members, customers can start selecting the sort of experience they want. It's customer choice, and we all know that's a good thing.

> 66Given the opportunity, each individual would have a different style, a personal way of operating that would distinguish him or her.99

> 66It's customer choice, and we all know that's a good thing.99

The alleged advantages of scripts are that they overcome the social incompe-tence of the staff and make sure that all key points are covered. If you are really employing socially incompetent staff in the key, customer-facing jobs there is something wrong with your recruitment (and quite possibly with your rates of pay for customer service staff). If the concern is to avoid items slipping through the net, look at alternatives to scripts. I used this example on giving customer service via call centres, and the Web, in my book *The Invisible Customer* (Kogan Page, 2000).

INVISIBLE SCRIPT

In the call centre, to provide a similar effect to the good public speaker unforced delivery, it would help to have both full scripts and keyword prompt. The agents should be taken through the full scripts, but then use the keyword prompts in their conversations. How those keywords are presented depends on your requirements. In this example there are both linear and mapped keyword. If you are prepared to take the time to produce them and give the agents fam iarity with them, mapped keywords are better, as it is easier to jump around diagram like this (Figure 2), better matching the non-linear nature of mo conversations. If the agents have some basic training in mapping (very useful fo taking notes when on the phone), they can draw their own maps which make easier to take in the map when using it live.

Script

Good morning/afternoon, my name is X from the BigCo Corporation. I'm callin you in response to your request for more information about our air-conditionin products. Could I get a little more information about your requirements?

- How many rooms will you need to provide air conditioning for?
- Can we take each of those rooms one at a time?
- What would you call the first one?
- Roughly how big is the room?
- Can you give me an idea of the number and size of windows?

The idea is that the keywords, especially in the visually flexible map format, act as a reminder to the customer contact staff to cover the relevant points, but don't get in the way of their natural conversational style. When I was writing *The Invisible Customer*, I recommended that the agents still be taken through full scripts as examples, but for a charismatic company I'm not sure that that is a good idea, as it will put into the agents' minds a suggestion of the sort of

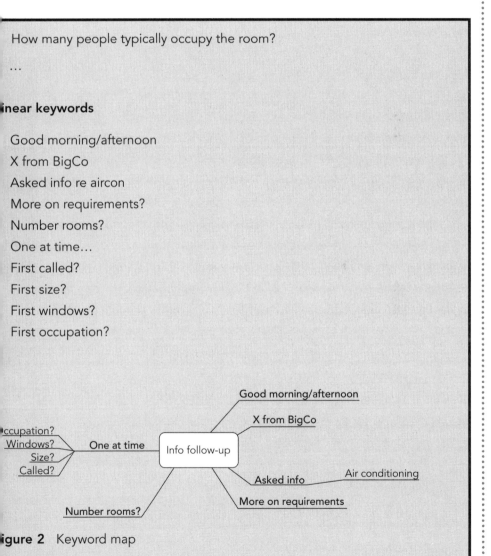

How many people typically occupy the room?

...

Linear keywords

Good morning/afternoon
X from BigCo
Asked info re aircon
More on requirements?
Number rooms?
One at time...
First called?
First size?
First windows?
First occupation?

Figure 2 Keyword map

delivery you want, even if that bears no relation to their natural style. Instead, for charisma, it is more effective to explore the message that the keywords are trying to get across and leave the agent (or whatever style of customer contact staff is involved) to get on with it. In such a context, the map shown in Figure 2 is too detailed. There's no need to hammer out specifics like Good morning, I'm X from BigCo. It would be better to be as general as 'greet and introduce self.' If you are more comfortable saying 'hi', accompanied by a warm, genuine smile, you are much more likely to come across well than by saying 'Good morning'.

ENTHUSIASTS IN ACTION

Many of us belong to clubs and societies. In them we mix socially with others who have similar interests. It's natural to feel an affinity for such people. If we are looking for ways to get customers to relate to our customer contact staff, it would help if the staff members had interests in common with the customers. That way it would be very natural to spark off a basic relationship.

This connection of interests can come in two ways. The customer contact staff could share an interest in the output of the business, or there could be something about the customer that the staff member spots that enables them to share a common enthusiasm that is unrelated to the business. Bearing this in mind, when customers are liable to arrive using their own transport, there's a lot to be said for being able to watch the customer all the way from their car or bike.

66If we are looking for ways to get customers to relate to our customer contact staff, it would help if the staff members had interests in common with the customers.99

66As long as it's the enthusiast that gets talking, rather than the staff member trying to use fictional knowledge, conversation will begin to flow.99

The vehicle itself could be a starting point. If it's something distinctive – a Harley or a classic British bike, a sports car or a custom creation – there's a chance to get enthusiastic. Harley-Davidson, one of the best companies in the world at milking its brand image, has been active in the organization of Harley-Davidson clubs and arranges special rallies where the fans can gorge themselves on Harley-Davidson merchandise. Even if the staff member isn't a fan herself, here's an opportunity where a little polite interest will work wonders. As long as it's the enthusiast that gets talking, rather than the staff member trying to use fictional knowledge, conversation will begin to flow.

Anything attached to a car or bike may also tell you something about the person who drives it that could be equally useful, but there's always a chance of getting it wrong – because they have borrowed someone else's car that carries a Greenpeace sticker, or the fish symbol was stuck on the back when the owner bought it. A less uncertain link, though, is the product or service that the customer has come to talk to you about. One way or another (even if it's a matter of hatred), the customer probably feels something about the product or service, or how it is going to be used. There will often be an opportunity to pick up on this, especially if the customer contact staff are enthusiasts themselves.

GOOD NEWS STORY

A FRIEND INDEED

'I must recommend Roger Taylor Classic Cars of Bournemouth who sold me an MGB of 24 years of age. They welcome me at a personal level when I have to go in. All customers are welcome to drop in to check out what's happening. Nothing is too much trouble. And it's not as if they are expensive for their services. I can't quote a specific example, as all my experience is that of being a friend who helps me out with my motoring hobby and only charges what they need to stay in business so they are there for me in the future.'

This enthusiastic recommendation from a customer says it all. He sees the company and its representatives as a friend. They are there for him. That company has charisma.

Businesses that centre on a hobby, like the classic cars example, can find it particularly easy to build up this sort of relationship with a customer, but there is hardly any product or service where it isn't possible to have *some* enthusiasm for it, or at least what it can do for you. Getting real enthusiasts as your customer contact staff is generally very helpful. The only possible danger is when enthusiasm runs away with the individual. I once bought a lawnmower from someone who could bore for his country on lawnmowers. He really loved lawnmowers. I genuinely appreciated the advice he gave – and trusted it – but there came a point when I could have done with a little less technology and a bit more sales processing. We got there in the end, but such enthusiasm may need a degree of reining in if the customers are really to appreciate the experience.

Don't assume, however, because you've got an enthusiast that they will relate to all your customers. It is the nature of enthusiasm to specialize. You might not be interested in old cars in particular, but be crazy about Austin Sevens. You might love books – as long as they aren't science fiction, crime or romances. Such specialization is fine as long as it doesn't cut across the demographics of your customers.

HORROR STORY

THE WRINKLED LIP

'Like many forty-somethings I have real problems when I go into a music store. Musical tastes are a lot freer and more eclectic now than even 20 years ago, but there is still a big age gap in tastes. This means, whenever I go up to the counter with a CD I just wait for the sneer from the teenage staff member (they always seem to be teenage). Okay, it's unlikely we are going to have many interests in common, but a little tolerance would not go amiss. It doesn't even matter if the server doesn't sneer – I'm anticipating it, and the effect is almost as bad.'

Once upon a time, when the music business was largely driven by singles, the youth market dominated sales. Things are different now, especially as most music

> ❝There is hardly any product or service where it isn't possible to have *some* enthusiasm for it.❞

shops sell a much wider range of goods – but the assistants, in a business where shared enthusiasms are very important – almost always only represent a tiny segment of musical taste. There's an opportunity there for someone. Compare bookshops, where there is quite often a much wider age range among the assistants.

THE COMMON GROUND

The common ground of interest, and the enjoyment of interacting with a real human being rather than a script-spouting clone, is enough to move the customer emotionally towards your customer contact staff. Your staff will have ceased to be pure 'them' and have some elements of 'us'. They will have started becoming 'people like us'. The alien nature of interacting with your business will have become a familiar process. Yet opening up the common ground isn't enough. It builds the bridge, but to cross it there needs to be trust.

GOOD NEWS STORY

AT LAND'S END

'The US mail-order company Land's End is famed for its policy of taking goods back, no excuses, whatever the reason. But they can go even further, giving the sort of response you expect from a real person, not a sales assistant.

'I remember I wanted to buy a shirt and top and wasn't sure from the catalog if they matched. I asked the woman on the phone if she could find out for me. She went and got the clothes right then and told me what she thought, how a stripe in one went well with the colour in the other. It's more than you expect over the phone.

'Another time they were out of stock of an item I wanted. They noticed that, though I'm from the States and was ordering from the US company, I was actually living in England for a while, so they contacted their British subsidiary, and they had one in stock and got it for me from there instead. So many companies just couldn't do that.'

66Opening up the common ground isn't enough. It builds the bridge, but to cross it needs trust.99

WORTHY OF TRUST

We have already seen how US retail chain Nordstrom has only one rule for its employees: 'Use your good judgement in all situations.' This is an example of the employer trusting the employee, but it's more than that. If it is done properly, the customer contact staff will act with integrity and that will inspire the remaining link of trust – that of the customer for the staff member. If circumstances show the customer that your staff are worthy of their trust, they will truly begin to seem to be friends. Without trust, everything else crumbles.

Usually trust is built up by a series of small interactions. It can take quite a while. Losing trust, though, is less evolutionary and more catastrophic. One incident can totally destroy trust, which might never be rebuilt. The most fundamental interaction that can generate trust is one where the staff member takes an action that is potentially detrimental to the individual or the company, putting the long-term relationship with the customer ahead of any immediate gain. It's what we do all the time with our children. Here are a few commercial examples that have happened recently:

- I walked into our village post office to send off a parcel. 'I'm glad you came in,' said the shopkeeper. 'Last time you came in I overcharged you. Here's your change.'

- In a similar incident in a fast food restaurant (see page 44), I was given a discount after being overcharged previously.

- I bought something from a small shopkeeper and realized I hadn't quite enough cash with me. 'Don't worry,' she said, 'pay me the rest next time you come in.' I did, and it was soon after.

- My wife went into a sports shop to buy a tent and some airbeds. The assistant pointed out that she could get the airbeds cheaper at a nearby catalogue store, but recommended she didn't go there for tents, as the catalogue store's much cheaper tents weren't properly waterproofed. They were more

66 'Use your good judgement in all situations.' 99

66 Without trust everything else crumbles. 99

playthings than real camping equipment. The sporting shop got her business for the tent, and in future.

This last example features a key ingredient of integrity in this type of relationship. The natural expectation of people who, after all, make a living from selling the products and services of their companies is that they will do anything

GOOD NEWS STORY

PUTTING OFF THE CUSTOMER

'A little while ago I went into Great Western Cameras in Swindon, and asked what was now available in digital cameras for around £400 [$600]. The answer was shocking at first. "I wouldn't sell you a camera in that price range," said the sales assistant. I was about to ask him what was wrong with my money when he went on. "One of the best manufacturers has just dropped the price of its cameras from £650 to £400. If you come back in a few days, I can do you a much better camera for £400 than I could today. I really wouldn't recommend buying anything now."

'Look at what he did. He turned away the chance to make an immediate sale. Taken in isolation this is madness – and sadly it's something that the sales assistants in many chain stores would not do, because it's push, push, push to move goods today. What the assistant did was to balance the value of the sale now against my long-term custom. I was very impressed that he had said that he wouldn't sell me a camera now, and that by going back in a few days I could get a much better one. I will go back, not just for that camera but for other purchases. And I have already passed on this story to several other would-be purchasers.'

66To make a sale whatever it takes means that integrity goes out of the window.99

66It's push, push, push to move goods today.99

to make a sale. This recipe for short-termism will inevitably put customers off and kill repeat business. It is giving the remaining lifetime value of the customer away to whoever wants it. Because to make a sale whatever it takes means that integrity goes out of the window. In these very special examples, though, the customer service staff appear to think that it's more important that the customer gets a good deal than that they get a sale straight away. Here's another example.

Here is a classic case of the customer contact staff putting my need above the immediate requirement to make a sale. The result – an increase in trust in the individual and the company that implicitly supports such behaviour. When marketing guru Jay Abraham speaks of ways to get more out of your customers, he doesn't encourage ripping them off for all they've got. Instead, to get that long-term business he recommends making sure that the customer's need comes first. That you genuinely help the customer, even if that means in the short term reducing your revenue from that customer. Like all the best structures, the trust that you gain this way is worth vastly more than the cost of building it.

ALLOWING INDIVIDUALITY

We have already looked at how trusting your staff is an essential part of giving them the ability really to deliver great customer service (see page 54). Giving the staff member the authority to act as an individual is part of that trust. If you really trust the individual, you can trust them to understand that they may need to keep some aspects of that individuality in check to avoid damaging the business or upsetting customers. You might have a trusted staff member who happened to be a naturist. You can allow her to display her individuality but still trust that she won't turn up for work naked without needing a company policy that says clothes must be worn at all time.

In my managerial career I frequently had members of staff who were definitely individuals. Occasionally I was accused by other managers of going

❝The customer's need comes first.❞

out of my way to collect oddballs. This simply wasn't true – for that matter, they weren't oddballs. What I tried to do was to get hold of staff I knew could achieve much more than the average. Such people often really appreciate their individuality, and part of gaining their respect was to give that individuality sufficient rein, on the understanding that I trusted them to do the right thing. There was one team leader, for instance, who hated suits and ties. One day I asked him to substitute for me at an important meeting. My boss was concerned. What if he turned up without a tie? While personally I felt that the world was unlikely to collapse in this event, I was able to point out that the team leader had a suit and tie on his coat rack, for just such occasions. So would I be instructing him to wear it? My boss still hadn't got the point. The team leader went to the meeting; the suit and tie were worn.

THE LIKING CHAIN

Customers will like you when you like the organization you are working for.

David Freemantle, consultant and author, in *What Customers Like About You*

This quote from David Freemantle is a frightening consideration for companies that believe in milking their staff for all they can get. As I write this, several well-known companies are cutting back harshly on staff. The atmosphere in these companies is bad. Rumours are rife. What were once popular organizations with their staff are now disliked and distrusted. The fine words in the annual reports ('People are our most important asset') have proved to be just that – fine words. In fact, people are proving to be their most disposable asset. And the outcome of this? As the staff like the companies less and less, the customers are starting to dislike the staff and their service. There is every possibility of producing a spiral of disaster.

I am not saying that you should never lay off staff. It is sometimes necessary. But the companies that have managed to generate this feeling of distrust and dislike internally have forgotten about the importance of individuality. In their panic to be seen by the stock markets to be ruthlessly cutting back on costs, they have treated people as faceless components – as figures on the balance sheet. And with the individuality they have lost the trust. It's like one of those irritating games where a stack of marbles are held up by sticks that you pull out one by one. Pulling out trust and individuality can send the whole pile crashing to the ground.

THE PERSONAL TOUCH

By allowing individuality we give our customer contact staff the opportunity to become real people. The sort of people who can give a personal touch. Dealing with our company doesn't have to be a bland, faceless experience any more. The ideal, the village store ideal, is that we turn to our friends and extol the virtues of 'Joe' or 'Sarah' or whoever we have dealt with. A real person, who has given advice, who we would turn to again, who puts a face on the business. (See the Hutchison Telecom story on page 61 for a good example of this in action.)

Sometimes the customer needs a little help along the way. Almost any business can provide that personal touch to at least some of it customers, some of the time. It would be unreasonable to expect to go into any branch of my bank and find my personal cashier there waiting for me – but not unreasonable to expect to find her in my usual branch. Or when I go in for a booked meeting. Remember the example of your doctor.

Even if you can't provide the personal touch to every individual every time, you can aim to make sure everyone gets it where possible, and your key customers get it whenever they deal with you. Some companies might argue that theirs is a special case. For instance, take an airline. You can't expect to deal with the same person on check-in, or have the same flight attendant each time. And yet a large airline's biggest spending customers probably put at least £250,000 a year its way. Would it be too unreasonable to have a dedicated flight

❝Sometimes the customer needs a little help along the way. ❞

attendant? Such a person might operate in the normal way, but have a standby requirement, should one of his or her key passengers be booked onto a flight, to be on that flight. As always there will be circumstances where it didn't work, but you could guarantee a familiar face on maybe half the flights the customer made. Wouldn't that make your service something special?

PEOPLE HELP PEOPLE

Probably the most noticeable difference between people and employees is that people help other people, employees don't. This seems a sweeping statement, but generally speaking, people will go out of their way to be helpful when someone else is in trouble. Employees all too often hide behind their uniforms and their job descriptions to say, 'This isn't what I'm here for.' If you can get you staff to move away from this position you can do so much for customer service.

The reluctance to help is often driven by the lack of trust we have already identified as a problem. It would help to know that this is the sort of behaviour that you are liable to rewarded for, rather than criticized by your manager for spending too much time on something that isn't your core job. Building that confidence is important, because it can really pay off.

GOOD NEWS STORY

I'LL TAKE CARE OF IT

'I flew into Los Angeles for a stay. I'd been up most of the night – I was worn out. When I got to the hotel there was no room for me, although it had been booked. While they were trying to get that fixed I went to pick up my rental car and that had been screwed up too. The hotel people were no help at all. They just weren't interested; car rental wasn't their problem. But the woman on the car rental desk took everything in hand.

❝Probably the most noticeable difference between people and employees is that people help other people, employees don't.❞

'She found a number for the representative of the travel company who had arranged the accommodation and the car. She got in touch with him, and made it clear he'd better get his finger out. She sorted out the hotel for me. She got a driver to take me back to the hotel, because she said I was clearly too tired to drive in a strange city. She sent the car round to the hotel in the morning.

'Now she was just the night manager of the car rental company. Most of this wasn't her problem. But did she make a difference.'

The fact is that once we get over the obsession with making our customer contact staff uniform clones we can provide a customer with a real person to deal with – an essential component of charisma.

66 Once we get over our obsession with making our customer contact staff uniform clones we can provide a customer with a real person to deal with. **99**

7 SURPRISE, SURPRISE!

Surprise can be a powerful weapon when developing charisma, just as it can in any other aspect of a relationship. It's a double-edged sword – the wrong kind of surprise can be upsetting, but pleasant surprises really increase your customers' enthusiasm for your company, and encourage them to tell their friends and relations just how great you are. This can be anything from a mundane change like a sudden price cut to something totally unexpected – the effect is surprisingly powerful.

YOU'LL NEVER GUESS...

Surprise is both powerful and dangerous. The concept of the surprise party is a classic example. When it goes right, the sudden transformation of a dull evening into a full-scale party can be euphoric. The organizers of the party clearly believe that it is going to be something special, or they wouldn't have gone to all that trouble. Yet sometimes the outcome can be anything but pleasant. The mechanics of the surprise – often involving a degree of deceit – can go wrong and be misinterpreted. When the surprise is sprung, the recipient sometimes reacts very negatively. Perhaps they were looking forward to a quiet evening. Perhaps they had planned something else. This is supposed to be for their benefit, but it's not what they want.

❝Surprise is both powerful and dangerous.❞

In planning a surprise for your customers, it's important to ensure that those potential negatives are expected and countered. If there is any misdirection along the way to ensure that the surprise isn't anticipated, care should be taken that it does not cause irritation. And be very aware of resistance to change of plans. When a customer is set on a particular course, it doesn't matter how exciting your alternative, there can be considerable resentment on being forced to change. From this viewpoint, the best surprises don't require the customer to look the other way while they are prepared, and don't require immediate action when the surprise is sprung, but give the customer a chance to get used to the idea.

SURPRISE CHANGES

Surprise is about things being different from the way you expect. So a prime opportunity in giving your customers a positive surprise is making an unexpected change – to the product, the store or any other aspect of the customer's relationship with the company.

HORROR STORY

A SORRY TAIL

The sort of surprise that turns out to be a nasty shock for the customer is illustrated well by the decision British Airways made in the late 1990s to transform the airline's aircraft livery by having different patterns from around the world on aircraft tails. It was a classic example of listening to the designer, rather than the consumer. The outcome was arguably a disaster.

The reasoning behind the change caused uproar in the UK. The argument was that BA was now a global carrier, with allegiance to a global market. To put ▶

66 Be very aware of resistance to change of plans... Give the customer a chance to get used to the idea. 99

66 Surprise is about things being different from the way you expect. 99

designs from around the world on the tails would stress this. Unfortunately, it's not what a lot of customers wanted. From ex-premier Margaret Thatcher down, British customers expressed a surprising amount of patriotic disgust. Perhaps more surprisingly, the concept was not too popular with non-British customers either. What many passengers were looking for in coming to British Airways was its distinctive Britishness. To do away with this left a bland global mess with no obvious character.

But it wasn't the reasoning alone that made this a bad idea. The fact is, the decorated tails *looked* a mess. Several of the designs looked as if graffiti artists had got into the hangar overnight and sprayed all over the tail. At airports, where the tail design is often used to identify the airline, BA aircraft became faceless unknowns. The trouble is, the airline had relied on designers' views alone. Just as catwalk fashion quite often looks ridiculous to the general public, but is made practical before it hits the high street, designer concepts for your business need to be passed through the twin filters of practicality and public response.

This was the sort of surprise the public would never accept – and it didn't. Within a couple of years, British Airways was reverting to a uniform livery. Sadly, the company didn't even have the grace to accept that the original decision had been a mistake. Note, by the way, that taking into account public response doesn't mean being swayed by initial reaction to change, which is almost always unfavourable. The previous BA change of livery had been criticized, but as the public saw the old and new alongside each other, they soon realized that the new, Landor-designed livery looked much better, making the old livery dated and ugly.

It's fine for surprises to shock, as long as they don't leave a bad taste in the mouth.

66 Designer concepts for your business need to be passed through the twin filters of practicality and public response. 99

Some elements of surprise change will almost always be welcomed. A surprise offer – reduced price, two for the price of one. Or more of the product for the same price. Anything that is simple enhancement of value for money will inevitably go down well. Other changes are less certain in their impact.

If you are uncertain of the impact of a surprise change, make sure that you think it through from the customers' viewpoint. Don't be swayed by designers and others with a vested interest in change. If possible, run the old and the new alongside each other for a while. You can monitor customer response, and give them a chance to see how (and if) the old is actually worse than the new. If the customer response remains uniformly negative, be prepared to pull the plug. Changes of look regularly cause initial customer disgruntlement, but are necessary to avoid an old-fashioned look. Again, if possible, maintain the old style in parts until the customers are won over. It usually only takes a few weeks if your change is a genuine improvement.

Some surprise changes are designed to cause the customer a degree of confusion. Take, for example, the supermarket technique of regularly changing the position of products within the store. The idea is that it will expose customers, who tend to have a habitual path through the store, to different products and will expand their shopping habits. That's fine, but again there is a balance. The very fact that customers have habitual paths means that they will expect to go to counter X and find the product they want. When they don't, they have to search and become irritated. Their shopping is slowed down. It might be to the store's benefit if the shopper's progress through the store is brought to a crawl, but it doesn't help the customer who is in a hurry.

❝It's fine for surprises to shock, as long as they don't leave a bad taste in the mouth.❞

The difficult decision from a customer service viewpoint is whether or not the customer can get any benefits from these sorts of changes. A facile argument is that they do benefit by being exposed to interesting new products they wouldn't otherwise have seen, but if you desperately need potatoes, it's no great consolation that you get the novelty of seeing star fruit and lychees. It would be more to the shopper's benefit, and would improve your store's charisma if

GOOD NEWS STORY

THEY LISTENED!

Taking the trouble to listen to your customers about a change they don't like can be a real plus. Cereal manufacturer Kellogg changed the name of a well-established cereal in the UK from Coco Pops to Choco Crispies. Like many manufacturers, they were probably trying to make product names uniform across national boundaries. But the change was unpopular, and remained so over at least a year. Rather than ignore its customers, Kellogg organized a phone poll using toll-free numbers. The majority voted for Coco Pops, and the old name was reinstated. This was a real boost for Kellogg's corporate charisma – here was a company that listened.

Contrast the sullen approach of confectionery company Mars, when the chocolate bar that had been called Marathon in the UK was renamed Snickers to bring it in line with other countries. Mars may have saved money by doing this, and strengthened the visibility of the international brand, but the UK customers didn't like it. In response Mars did nothing. And many customers in the UK still remember and resent the change, many years later. This is the sort of surprise that people don't like. The implication is that the global brand image is more important than the customer – not a healthy message.

things stayed where they were expected to be. That doesn't mean you can't have slots alongside popular lines through which you rotate novel products, but the customer's familiarity is a powerful attractor. One of the reasons I generally shop in one supermarket rather than its competitor is that I know where everything is. If I go in the competitor I can't find half the things I want. The more 'my' supermarket messes around with floor layouts, the more likely I am to defect to the competition, as I would then be lost wherever I shop. You don't make people comfortable by getting them lost.

UNEXPECTED GIFTS

If change is a double-edged sword, it's much harder to go wrong with surprise gifts. Price cuts are fine, and operate as a subset of the gift, but the human mind is strange and we nearly always give more value to a gift than cash. It's true of birthday presents and it's true of gifts to customers. For these purposes, a certificate or voucher is probably the least beneficial of all – it's effectively cash that can only be spent in particular places. At least, that's true of cash discount vouchers (£5 off your next visit to our shop, provided you come in the next three days), but not as much of product or service vouchers that can be exchanged for a specific gift without any payment. Whether it's a free meal or a free toy, such vouchers (especially if they carry appropriate illustrations) can be a powerful incentive.

These types of surprise are under-used at the moment. Probably the best exponents are burger chains, who frequently use scratch cards and other devices to give you the random opportunity to win a surprise each time you shop with them. This is also a very effective mailshot weapon, with one proviso. We are all familiar with the mass mailing that announces that you (yes, you!) have already been selected to win a fabulous mystery prize. Which inevitably turns out to be a plastic lemon squeezer or something equally useless. Surprise gifts have to

❝The customer's familiarity is a powerful attractor... You don't make people feel comfortable by getting them lost.❞

❝Surprise gifts have to awaken the customers' interest, not their cynicism.❞

awaken the customers' interest, not their cynicism. With an increasingly sophisticated customer base, some care has to be taken not to patronize with gifts – and to make sure that they are properly targeted.

GOOD NEWS STORY

THE POPCORN INITIATIVE

In this example, the surprise gift is a very practical one for parents.

Roush Hardware in Dublin, Ohio, is a small-town hardware store that thrives despite the competition from big players. 'The first thing you notice when you go in is a raised area, almost like a church pulpit. There is always someone there to help. You are asked 100% of the time "Can I help you find anything?" and again if it looks like you're having trouble.

'As a woman I sometimes find I'm made to feel like a ninny when I ask for help in a hardware store. I explained in Roush's just what I wanted to do. They went through it step by step with me and wrote down what I needed to get. They told me what the options were and said if I needed any help to call them. If there was anything it turned out I didn't need, I could just take it back. The people there are very knowledgeable and give help proactively.

'Oh, and there's a popcorn machine to keep the kids occupied when you need to get things done. It's like everything a Mom and Pop store should be.'

SURPRISING FORGOTTEN CUSTOMERS

Gifts can come in particularly useful for surprising customers who seem to have forgotten all about you. It's surprisingly easy for the customers to forget you – in fact, it's human nature. We use a shop or a restaurant or a service regularly. But for one reason or another our usage drops. We want a change, or simply don't bother to go any more.

"Gifts can come in particularly useful for surprising customers who seem to have forgotten all about you."

Such customers represent a huge opportunity. Assuming they've had a reasonable experience with you before, especially if it involved a touch of charisma, it will be much easier to win them back than attempting to attract entirely new customers. So surprise them. Send them a voucher for a free meal or small purchase. Give them their next service free. It might seem like unnecessary expenditure, but a small (in terms of their potential lifetime value) expenditure will reap big benefits when you get them back and retain them – and all the evidence shows that a surprisingly high proportion of old customers will come back, and keep on coming back.

Doing this requires two things – courage to take a risk and a well-maintained record of who your customers are. If you aren't prepared to take good risks, and this is an excellent one, you shouldn't be in business. If you don't have records of your customers (and hence can't identify the customers who have stopped using you in the last year), it's time to start making sure you get some.

CREATIVITY IS SEXY

Bearing in mind the idea that surprise is about things being different from expectation, creativity is an important element in this component of charisma. For much of our lives we operate in a rut, moving up and down a familiar, well-trodden path. That's fine when you don't need more. But it's a tight restriction when there's a need for change. Seeing things differently from 'the way we've always done it' is what creativity is all about – it's the power behind surprise.

The most popular approach when trying to develop a surprise – or any other business idea – is brainstorming. This is a real pity, as it's not a particularly effective way of generating ideas. The inventor of brainstorming, Alex Osborn, never intended it to be used in this way. He saw brainstorming as part of a two-stage process. The first stage (which typically isn't carried out) was to use a technique to push you out of your box, getting you thinking in a different way and generating new ideas. The second stage was to use brainstorming to collate,

66Seeing things differently is what creativity is all about – it's the power behind surprise. **99**

combine and enhance these ideas. It's rather like expecting a gun to fire without a trigger – with brainstorming alone, there's nothing to start off the process.

Luckily, Osborn and his successors produced a wide range of techniques that will repeatedly and reliably stimulate creative thought. A typical creativity technique pushes the participants out of conventional trains of thought, into a new direction. As an example, one of Osborn's original techniques was reversal. This works by taking a fundamental aspect of the requirement and reversing it. By looking at the implications of the reversal, you can begin to see new possibilities in the real world. Say, for example, you were looking for new ways to communicate with your customers. Reversal might say, 'How can you avoid communication with your customers?' With a number of possibilities explored, these options are then examined for their implications for the real requirement. For example, one way you might avoid communication is by putting a paper bag over your head. This might make you think of a number of communication options. You might put messages on shopping bags (details of an upcoming campaign, for instance). You could put messages on hats (either to be worn by shop assistants or to give to the customers). You could put a giant paper bag on the store with the message on. You could send your customers a bag of goodies to get the message across. And so on...

This is not the place to go into the mechanics of enhancing creativity in any depth. There several books on creativity listed on page 212 – a good all-round book as a starting point is *Imagination Engineering* (Brian Clegg and Paul Birch). The point is, however, that creativity is an essential part of this and several other components of charisma, and it's not enough to wish for it, or even to brainstorm. If you want to take your creativity seriously, you need to put some conscious effort into enhancing it.

❝A typical creativity technique pushes the participants out of conventional trains of thought, into a new direction.❞

❝If you want to take your creativity seriously, you need to put some conscious effort into enhancing it.❞

BEING DIFFERENT

NORDSTROM IS DIFFERENT

'Everyone talks about Nordstrom stores being "King of CS". I was shopping with my son and bought him a pair of Doc Marten's – the most popular school shoe for the 11-year-old crowd. He was trying on sizes and accidentally put an 8 and a 9 size shoe in his box. Away we went having purchased them and didn't realize the error until a week or so at home. By the time we realized the mistake I had thrown away the receipt, the box was gone, and there was no proof of any kind that the shoes had been purchased at Nordstrom. Well, we went back to the store and they immediately accepted the shoes, and had three sales associates working to find a new pair in my son's size. It was the type of experience that makes me want to buy all our family's shoes at Nordstrom.'

The Nordstrom story proves that surprise doesn't have to be extreme or flashy. Here the surprise is simply being different from the way shops are. We know that if we take back unboxed products without a receipt there will be a fuss. Not at Nordstrom. Surprise!

Since surprise is about defeating expectations, one simple approach to generating surprise is to be different from your competitors, to challenge expectations on what your particular type of business is like. Exactly what form that surprise can take will vary hugely from business to business. As an exercise in exploring surprise, spend a few moments jotting down the key attributes of your business. What does everyone expect in a business like yours? Then look at some totally different businesses. What do they do that you don't? Is there anything you can use? Finally, let your mind wander through different pleasurable experiences from your customers' viewpoint. Are there aspects of

> ❝One simple approach to generating surprise is to be different from your competitors.❞

the ways your customers enjoy themselves that can be brought into your business and customer service?

Let's take a concrete example – an accountancy firm. The key attributes might be reliability, timeliness, professionalism and confidentiality. Now think of a few unrelated businesses – perhaps an ice-cream parlour, a funeral director's and an advertising agency. Some randomly picked attributes might be brightness, choice of flavours, popularity with youth, quiet efficiency, 24-hour operation, energy and off-the-wall originality. You could then consider each of these attributes applied to the accountancy. Sometimes the application could be direct. Many small businesses do their paperwork in the evenings and at weekends – a 24-hour help line would be very beneficial for such customers. Others might be indirect. You might not aim for the youth market, but you could realize that a fair percentage of your clients might be working mothers with young children. What do you offer to keep the children amused when they come to see you?

Applying the final step of examining how customers enjoy themselves to this example, a lot of your accountancy clients might like playing golf. What do they like about this? Perhaps the exercise, the opportunity to get away from the phone, socializing with peers. You might then be able to make changes to make your business more attractive in these ways. Or again by indirect association – getting away from the mobile phone might be turned on its head – could you offer up-to-the-minute stockmarket advice via a mobile phone messaging service?

The specifics aren't really the point here. Time and time again when looking at competitive advantage, the experts come down on differentiation as a major factor. By looking for opportunities explicitly to make a difference from the standard expectations of your business, you can differentiate effortlessly. And the element of surprise will enhance your customers' feeling that there is something special about your firm. Here's a company that doesn't stick to the everyday – you keep getting pleasant surprises.

66 Time and time again when looking at competitive advantage, the experts come down on differentiation as a major factor. 99

BEING FUN

As we've already seen in looking at the realities of having a star head up the company, there has traditionally been an uncomfortable match between business and fun. Whether it's an offence to the Anglo-Saxon, Protestant work ethic or something completely different, fun is something that most businesses outside the entertainment industry avoid. We might make customers feel comfortable in our banks or supermarkets or business consultancies (or at least minimize discomfort), but there is little chance of a customer having a good time.

Just occasionally that is a very sensible thing. Some places of business are about the sad aspects of life and we don't necessarily want to be having a great time. But there are plenty more where we could have fun without degrading the function of the business. Why shouldn't many of our everyday experiences as customers be more fun?

GOOD NEWS STORY

TOWELLING MASTERPIECES

'I'm always amazed at the customer service in Disneyworld, but last October we stayed in one of the resort hotels for the first time. The maid built little animals out of the hand towels, a dog, a rabbit and so on, getting more elaborate through the stay, until there were monkeys hanging from a rope even. She had stickers for eyes and everything. Our children were writing her thank you notes – we actually looked forward to getting back to the room to see what she'd done today. It might be something small, but it's the detail that counts.'

In employing fun as a surprise tactic, remember that it isn't a one-size-fits-all commodity. All too often, the sort of fun that appeals to five-year-olds – dressing up in silly clothes while being hit with balloons and coated in gunk, for

❝There has traditionally been an uncomfortable match between business and fun.❞

example – is assumed to be the appropriate level for any customer. It doesn't have to be like this. However, it is also worth pointing out that humour and fun is very much a gut-level reaction, and so it shouldn't be too surprising if it is often less intellectual than we might expect.

For that matter, having fun doesn't always equate to humour. It could be a matter of having a good time, rather than a boring one. Looking at ways you can make going to the bank more like having coffee and donuts with friends. Making a trip to the supermarket more like walking round an oriental bazaar. The possibilities are there with the appropriate creativity. And what better surprise than one that makes a normal, routine necessity into fun?

66In employing fun as a surprise tactic, remember that it isn't a one-size-fits-all commodity.99

66Having fun doesn't always equate to humour.99

66What better surprise that one that makes a normal, routine necessity into fun?99

8 TECHNICAL WIZARDRY

If there is any sexism to charisma, this is the one that is aimed particularly at the men. There's something very appealing about technical wizardry and the ability to turn out gee-whiz products. It's often a hard lesson for the me-too manufacturer, but it is one that companies like Sony have demonstrated will win.

GEE-WHIZZERY

Sometimes you just look at a product and go 'wow!' You must have one. It doesn't really matter what it does or whether you have a genuine use for it, it goes straight for the gut and says 'buy me'. For a lot of people (and it seems particularly a lot of men), gadgets, gizmos and extreme technology have a fascination out of all proportion to their genuine value. Some would argue that the whole space industry is essentially a matter of big boys' toys – the ultimate in gee-whizzery.

Take a GPS satellite location system. One of those handy little gadgets will tell you exactly where you are in the world, down to a few metres. While they can be effective for navigation when linked to a computer mapping system, the GPS device in isolation is practically useless for most of us. Yet almost

❝Sometimes you just look at a product and go 'wow!' You must have one.❞

every man feels a siren song when faced with such a device that seductively says, 'You want me.'

Sometimes today's super-gadgets become everyday; sometimes they will remain on the wacky periphery, but there is a stream of devices that fall readily into this bracket. Looking back over the last 20 or so years, sure-fire gee-whiz products have included PCs, digital watches (no, really), CDs, the Walkman, Minidisk, cellular phones, wide screen TV... and many, many more. Some are mundane. The refined end of the corkscrew market is full of fascinating gadgets. Others add a variant to a commonplace. There's nothing exciting *per se* about a clock. But make it a clock that is updated by radio from an atomic clock, always keeping perfect time, and you've got yourself a winner. Even low tech can produce super-gadget success, as typified by the wind-up radio.

Whole companies, both mail-order and retail outlets, specialize in the delight of gadgetry. Sometimes these companies get it wrong, confusing gimmick with gadget. An amazing plastic whatsit for removing the cores of apples might be very useful (perhaps), but it doesn't have the gee-whiz touch. Don't worry, though, that you aren't that kind of company. Neither is Sony or Nokia or Braun, but it doesn't stop them turning out a host of stylish gadgets.

THE PILOT SYNDROME

One of the fascinating things about aiming to appeal to gadget lovers is that some of the classic rules of design go out of the window. I call this the pilot syndrome. Many years ago, when I still occasionally designed computer programs, I was involved with a group of pilots in prototyping some software that they would use to bid for trips around the world. This was PC software to use from home. My natural inclination was to make the design as simple and clear as possible. They didn't like the result.

> 66 The refined end of the corkscrew market
> is full of fascinating gadgets. 99

> 66 One of the fascinating things about aiming to appeal to
> gadget lovers is that some of the classic rules of design go
> out of the window. 99

As an experiment, I loaded lots of information and controls into a single screen – much more than would normally be acceptable in a good user interface. They loved it. While I have no scientific evidence to back up this theory, my suspicion is that pilots, used to interacting with the vast array of switches and dials in an aircraft flight deck, actually wanted a more complex user interface. They feel comfortable about having lots of information thrown at them at once, with arrays of controls immediately available. It's what they are used to; they like it.

To some extent, this pilot syndrome extends into realm of gadgets. The normal rules of design sometimes have to be forgotten. While the elegant lines of Bang & Olufsen's stereo equipment are very appealing (and might push them into the classic design products referred to on page 68), they haven't got what it takes in the gadget world. To see the pilot syndrome in action, you only have to observe a man and woman looking at watches in a jeweller's window.

Many women will prefer the slim, minimalist designs, which just about tell the time if you are lucky. A surprising number of men are attracted to the big, chunky watches, not so much for the manly weight of the thing but the fact that it has 15 different dials, can tell you the barometric pressure and can be used as a TV remote control. Even men whose social condition has inclined them to like slim, elegant watches will feel a pang of longing when faced with a 1/100 of a second stopwatch feature, or the ability to download diary appointments from the PC.

You don't have to go for the pilot syndrome when attracting customers by using the appeal of gadgetry. With the right functionality, simple design can still win customers over. But it's worth bearing in mind that this anomaly exists before you dismiss the button from the CD player that automatically splits the tracks so they can be recorded on two sides of a cassette (there is such a button on my CD player). Perhaps the VCR manufacturers who produce remote handsets with a simple version on one side and a complex one on the other have the right idea.

66A particular joy of using gadgetry to make customers fall for your products is that you can often tap into a part of the market that wasn't even there before.**99**

THEY DON'T KNOW THEY WANT IT

A particular joy of using gadgetry to make customers fall for your products is that you can often tap a part of the market that wasn't even there before. The customers won't have asked for your gadget, or even necessarily appreciate what it can do for them until they see it in action, but once word starts spreading, they will discover that it's something they've wanted all their life.

A good example of this is the Walkman. While there is some historical evidence that the Walkman was developed when an executive came in with a Walkman-sized block of wood and said, 'Build me something this big I can use to listen to music,' I like to imagine an R&D team doing a presentation to the board. 'We've invented the Walkman,' they say. 'Oh, yes,' say the board members, 'what's that?' The R&D team confer. 'Well, it's a cassette player. You can strap it on your waistband and walk around listening to it.'

The board members, thinking of the typical half-a-briefcase-sized cassette recorder of the time, don't take long to consider this proposal. 'So you've got this cassette recorder, only it won't record it just plays. And you think people are going to strap it to themselves and walk around? It won't work. It'll be too bulky and too heavy. People won't want to inflict their music on other people. And they all want to record. And who wants to listen to music while they are walking? No one has ever asked for anything like this. No one at all. Anyway, we couldn't schedule an all-new product into the production lines for the next three years.' Luckily, Sony doesn't operate like this.

When you are dealing with a new gadget you can throw away your market research. Your customers really don't know that they want it. What you want is to be able to generate that sense of surprise, to get their eyes widening, to have them tell their friends, 'It's so cool.' One of the advantages this 'no one knew they wanted it' effect has is that the product has a better chance of getting exposure through the regular media. A mobile phone isn't newsworthy, but a mobile phone with an animated newsreader on its screen (or whatever) is.

66When you are dealing with a new gadget you can throw away all your market research.99

TECHNICAL CREATIVITY IS SEXY TOO

Everything that was said about creativity in the previous chapter applies equally well in the technical field. Creativity techniques and methodologies can be incredibly effective at developing new products and adding a new twist to an old product. Although a gadget can appeal from pure pilot syndrome, usually it's something new about it that catches the eye. This innovation has to come from somewhere – and it's the innovation that takes the product into the charisma zone.

Bear in mind that creativity here, as so often elsewhere, can be about seeing something commonplace in a different setting. Taking an idea from a whole different business or technology or type of product can produce the sort of technological innovation that pushes a gadget into a customer's imagination and affection. Some sources – space technology, computing – are applicable across a huge range of applications from flashlights to phones. But don't restrict yourself to hi-tech sources. The roller-ball deodorant applicator was inspired by the ballpoint pen. Something you see in a plant nursery could inspire a whole new range of home gadgets. The opportunities for creativity are huge, provided the first step of bothering to do something about it is taken.

PLOTTING COOL

To be successful with a gadget you need to be able to predict in advance (or at least have a good shot at predicting in advance) just what is going to appeal to the consumer. To plot out the cool products at the design and development stage. No one is going to get it right every time. Sir Clive Sinclair was a gadget-lover's hero with his tiny matchbox radios and small affordable computers. Yet his C5 electric micro-car failed to achieve that coolness factor. But failure should not be seen as a negative. You can plot out products that are more likely than

❝Creativity can be about seeing something commonplace in a different setting.❞

❝The opportunities for creativity are huge, provided the first step of bothering to do something about it is taken.❞

most to be accepted, but part of the process has to be learning from failure and advancing. The mark of success in this market is just how fast you can get a product out, fail, learn from that failure and move on.

The most important arbiter of cool in gadgets is the gut. There is no point trying to be entirely logical. You can't say: 'Product X was great, and product Y was great, and product Z was great, so we're going to make a new gadget that's a combination of the three.' This sort of logical approach might be used to devise options, but the decision has to come down to gut feel. Not objective numbers, but a real feel for how the public will react. Make a little video of the product in a shop window and in use. Does the sight of the product in the window make you want to dash in and buy one? Does the user look or feel stupid? Does the sight of someone with the product make you feel envious? Get people who aren't involved in the product's development to take this test – they will be less biased.

It's hard to imagine that the C5 was put through a test like this. You only have to see someone driving it in traffic to realize the problems. Cool it is not.

One resource that can be very effective in plotting coolness is the response of professional reviewers. Most magazine have reviewers who look at products before they are finished to write them up for their magazines. Get a bunch of reviewers involved early in the project (with a non-disclosure agreement). Get feedback. See how much competition there is to get hold of a limited number of trial products. See how many would like to see the finished product – if the trial product doesn't excite them, there won't be much interest in getting hold of the final version.

❝The mark of success in this market is just how fast you can get a product out, fail, learn from that failure and move on.❞

❝The most important arbiter of cool in gadgets is the gut.❞

❝If the trial product doesn't excite there won't be much interest in getting hold of the final version.❞

NOT FOR EVERYONE

There is no doubt that gadgetry is, for some, an element of charisma. You've only got to watch a James Bond movie to be convinced of this. But of all the components, this is probably the most sensitive to the customer's own makeup. As you move up the age groups there is an increasing resistance to techno-toys. Most teens and twenties of either sex will find them attractive, but as the audience gets older, a negative reaction kicks in with some of the population.

For these people gadgetry is a turn off. They don't like it. It might be that they are more comfortable with a 'natural', knit-your-own-yoghurt world and the high tech doesn't sit comfortably with their alternative lifestyle. It might be that they don't understand technology and are frightened of it. Or they may simply be bored by it. It's important to be aware of this grouping – but it's no reason for ignoring the potential of gadgetry. Just make sure that this component of charisma is optional, and the choice is down to the customer.

AIM AT TEENS; MOTIVATE ADULTS

It's arguable that the appeal of gadgets is a leftover from our teens. The response comes from the part of us that never grows up, the part that seems stronger in men than women. A truly successful gadget would make a teenager drool, but would actually be bought by adults. The basic appeal of the product has to hit that teenage interest level, while the packaging and marketing needs more sophistication.

This isn't to exclude the teenager. In an increasingly affluent society, they will buy such products too. But the adult will be put off by pure teenage packaging and marketing. It's a delicate balance that I think the computer games market has got all wrong, where the phone market has got it right. Many, many adults enjoy playing computer games, but hate the marketing of games in shops and magazines, where they have a solidly teen presentation. Internet selling may

❝A truly successful gadget would make a teenager drool, but would actually be bought by an adult.❞

change things a little, but it would be interesting to see whether the games market could be segmented more by also selling computer games in a more adult-oriented setting.

GOOD NEWS STORY

GAMING IN THE POCKET

Games on phones are a good example of the effectiveness of gadgetry at selling. The pocket phone is an ideal opportunity to use technology's siren song. A business colleague (an accountant, and otherwise perfectly normal) is in love with his phone because it has a game on it that he can play competitively with someone else who has the same phone. Childish, maybe, but it sells.

If you can get that balance right, the gadget can be a great way to enhance the customer's feelings about your company and your products. It doesn't work in every market, but it certainly extends far beyond the market for pure gadgets themselves. The gadgetry appeal of GPS route mapping in a car or intelligent circuitry in a microwave is already well established. Other markets are still wide open. The clothing market's only real exposure to date has been flashing lights in trainers. So much more could be done.

The same could go for almost any product area. Even services can be combined with gadgetry, whether it's clever devices in airline seats or Internet banking. The chances are that gadgets could help your business win the customer's affection.

> 66If you can get that balance right, the gadget can be a great way to enhance the customer's feelings about your company and your products.99

66The chances are that gadgets could help your business win the customer's affection.99

THEY'RE MINE, ALL MINE

If our aim is to make the customers feel positive about our company, it would help if they consider it to be *their* company. This can be achieved through formal means such as shareholding or informal means such as providing visible control over company direction.

PRIDE IN OWNERSHIP

We like what's ours. We don't like it when someone else criticizes our family or our car – we might do it ourselves, but we don't like anyone else to do so. This appeal can be extended to companies and products, if the customer can be brought to think of it as 'our product', 'our company'. And such bonds can be very strong. It is years now since I worked for British Airways, but I still feel inclined to defend the airline when it is criticized. It remains 'my' airline.

A sense of ownership brings loyalty and the inclination to recommend to other people. What is more, of all the components of charisma, it is one of the easiest to engineer. It really isn't that difficult to give people that feeling of ownership of your company. Yet very few companies bother to do it. It's almost as if board members are worried that increasing the sense of ownership (and by implication participation) will decrease their personal power, and so they resist this move, however much it is going to win over customers.

> 66A sense of ownership brings loyalty and the inclination to recommend to other people.99

SHOWERING SHARES

The traditional form of ownership in public companies is through the use of shares. It's a convenient mechanism for allocating a sense of ownership with very little danger of losing control. Individual shareholders provide few inconveniences for the company (unless they make a scene at the annual general meeting) but they do have an inevitable sense of buy-in. It's almost a licence to print your own money. Yet tying customers in with shares is something that very few companies have tried. It's more common with employees (though much less common than it should be), but not so with customers. When providing shares to customers, however, it is important to learn from the experiences of both employee schemes and shareholders in general.

Many employee share schemes provide an object lesson in how not to get value out of the exercise. I have heard companies complain that the share scheme had not had the desired effect of tying the staff into the fortunes of the company. Instead, the shares were just regarded as a cash bonus, to be sold at the first practical opportunity. When I ask such companies just what they did to support the share scheme in terms of information and education, I generally get blank looks. The employees got a share certificate, and as shareholders they got an annual report and accounts. What more did they want? They could read the *Wall Street Journal*, couldn't they?

I exaggerate a little, but the sad fact is that such companies are simply giving money away with no benefit accruing. It's not enough to dole out shares. Similarly, shareholders in general aren't given enough to tie them to the success and failure of the company. They get their certificates. They get dividends. If they are lucky, they get some form of voucher giving discounts on the company products. And of course they get the magnificent report and accounts. But nothing to interest and excite them. Nothing to give them a feeling of taking part. If you think the report and accounts does that, think again. We'll revisit the report and accounts in a moment. But it is worth giving serious consider-

66 **When providing shares to customers, it is important to learn from the experiences of both employee schemes and shareholders in general.** 99

ation first to whether or not there's any point in taking this action. Can the person in the street understand enough about what's going on to buy into your business emotionally?

I would argue that they can. These same people can handle lottery draws or betting odds. They can manage a household budget or keep a car on the road. They aren't incompetent idiots, but many of them will also not be accountants. Neither will they necessarily be experienced business people. If you tailor your approach to them, however, they can not only understand shares and their significance, but feel very much that your company belongs to them.

REPORT TIME

Let's get back to the report and accounts, your annual vehicle for keeping your shareholders informed. A typical corporate report and accounts is a glossy brochure with swathes of elegant pictures. It talks of the broad product ranges. Of the assets gained and sold. Of major changes to the business. And it has plenty of pages of near-incomprehensible numbers. I've two degrees, one in physics, the other in operational research, a maths-based discipline, and my eyes still glaze over at the sight of the endless tables of numbers, the profit and loss accounts, the balance sheets of an annual report. Intellectually I can handle them, but emotionally I skate over the surface. I can't *feel* what they mean for me and for the company. If you are an accountant, fine, they're meat and drink, but to normal human beings, the target audience of our exercise, they have little value.

The first stage of making shares a real emotional tie to the company is to redesign the report and accounts totally. Get rid of the balance sheets and profit and loss accounts and all those interminable tables of numbers. When you've picked up your accountant off the floor and applied the smelling salts, he will point out that you can't do this. There is a legal requirement to have certain information in there.

❝Can the person in the street understand enough about what's going on to buy into your business emotionally?❞

Fine. Put them in an appendix, separately printed on cheap paper. After all, no one but accountants will look at them, so why waste money on fancy presentation? Now let's get to business on the rest of the document.

Start again from scratch. Make sure the people who write the report are journalists, not accountants or line managers or even your in-house communications department. (You may think by now that I've got it in for accountants. Not at all. They just aren't the right people to communicate with normal human beings. They would be much better locked in large, airy rooms and left to their own devices.)

Fine, have your glossy presentation and nice pictures, but always drive the stories from the shareholder's viewpoint. 'What does it mean to me as a shareholder and customer?' should be in the mind of the writer every time. You might think that the best thing about a merger with another company is an entry into the South American market, or an improvement in your debt to equity ratio – your shareholder/customer may see the most important things are that they can get a wider range of discounted products, and that they are now (note *they* are now) involved in a project to save a patch of rainforest.

Pitch your text at the intelligent end of tabloid journalism, and remember journalism's golden rules. The headline (you don't have headlines? Why not?) should attract the eye and intrigue the reader. The first sentence should summarize the key aspects of the piece. Make sure there's plenty of human interest. Where there are figures, present them with plenty of graphics and explanation of the consequences. Throw in a few associated features. If you are a textile firm, you could have a feature on London Fashion Week (and the part you played). And why not include a 'something for me' section too – a competition, perhaps. Your aim should be to make the report and accounts something your customer/shareholders look forward to reading, not binning.

❝Your aim should be to make the report and accounts something your customer/shareholder looks forward to reading, not binning.❞

BEYOND THE REPORT EVENT HORIZON

If you limit yourself to the annual report, however, you are still missing the whole point of this exercise. Those people out there have two roles. They are customers and they are shareholders. We want to make use of the shareholder relationship to give the customers a sense of ownership, to the extent that they think of you as 'their' company and act accordingly. True charisma. To make this happen, sending out a single document a year, however glossy and thrilling, is grossly ineffective. The more the customer/shareholder knows about what is happening, the more they will feel connected. So communicate. And keep communicating.

At the very least quarterly, and quite possibly bi-monthly or even monthly, you should be in touch with your shareholders. Keeping them up to date with what is happening. Always reminding them that you are their company. Continuing to use the customer-centred viewpoint. Not great boasts about your company's achievements – boasting is boring for everyone but the boaster – but explorations of the impact of your actions on the customer's world. And although your customers aren't only motivated by self-interest, each mailing should have something that is purely for them. A goody; a treat.

The form this takes should vary from month to month. You might have competitions and draws. Vouchers and discount benefits. Opportunities to bring friends into the scheme. Tours of your facilities. Chances of taking a trip abroad to see where your raw materials come from. Free samples. Free tickets for the movies when you've got product placement in them, or discount vouchers for magazines that you advertise in. Pile on the benefits of being associated, always reinforcing the message: 'This is your company.'

Remember also that communication is two-way. A later chapter is all about communication with your customers, but in this special sense of communicating with shareholders, give them a chance to communicate back. To say what they think outside the formal and stifling environment of the AGM. Making sure, of

❝Boasting is boring for everyone but the boaster.❞

course, that anything they say is taken seriously. These are both customers and shareholders. They deserve better than a form letter, or a 'thank you, we'll think about it'. Sometimes they will be right – be prepared to take note and change the way you do things. And always get back to them promptly to say what is happening (even if it is nothing).

One way you can facilitate this is to set up a shareholder-only Web site. Give them access to a protected site where they can wallow in shareholder information and contribute to a bulletin board that is also contributed to by senior staff from your company. And once again, give them some incentives, some goodies for using the site. It's all part of the glue that will bind them to you.

SIGNING UP SHAREHOLDERS

The previous few sections have assumed that you have got your customers to become shareholders. You need to get from here to there. A good initial route, if you have such a scheme, is your loyalty card holders. Loyalty cards don't feature much in this book, because there's nothing charismatic about them. The last thing a loyalty card does is engender loyalty. But they do provide a good basis for a list of the sort of people who could be encouraged into becoming shareholders. Depending on your business, you might consider your mailing list, or club members, or any other vehicle you have for identifying regular clients.

When it comes to allocating shares, probably the best basis is to give a few free and have an extra allocation that can be bought at under the current share price. These should be tied into an appropriate scheme that limits their sale for a period of time. You need some time to build a relationship, to develop a sense of ownership. And, importantly, keep the process going. You will have new loyalty card customers (or whatever). Give them an opportunity too.

As we have already established, I am neither an accountant, nor a lover of accounting. There are probably half a dozen technical holes that a good accountant

❝The last thing a loyalty card does is engender loyalty.❞

can shoot in this proposal. But that would miss the point. It can be fine-tuned to fit your business and any legal requirements – but it is just a matter of tuning.

One interesting approach to customer shareholding that emerged with a number of ISPs (Internet service providers), the companies that give dial-up access to the Internet, is using a promise of shares to get customers to use their services. In the UK, such companies often operated a business model where the customer paid nothing to the ISP for using their service. Revenue was generated from a cut of the telephone call charge made by the phone company, and advertising on the ISP's home page. There was a flood of ISPs operating this model, so there was a need to provide an extra carrot to encourage customers to sign up.

The idea that emerged was to offer each signed-up user who made regular use of the connection a number of virtual shares in the company that would be converted to actual shares in the event of floatation. Of itself, this does not give the customer buy-in or a feeling of ownership. The ISP would have to go through the same process as any other company to win and maintain that condition. And the value of the shareholding is watered down initially while the shares remain virtual. But it was still an interesting new slant on buy-in through share ownership that could stimulate some alternative approaches, especially for companies that aren't public. If you don't have publicly available shares, why not issue your own equivalent? You would have to call them something else, but the effect could be the same, without all the legal framework of the share process. The ISP example may be short term as the UK moves more to unmetered phone calls, but the opportunity to use virtual shares is an interesting consideration.

ASKING WHAT THEY WANT

If shareholding is the most formal way to give your customers a feeling of ownership, the other extreme is so simple that it seems almost ridiculous. The more you ask your customers what they want – and give them what they ask for when it is practical – the more they will feel that you are 'their' company. If you are in retail, when did you last ask your customers what they wanted you to stock? It would be so easy to make a big thing of it, yet it is rarely done. Variants could be applied to almost any line of business.

This isn't a blanket acceptance that the customer is always right. Inevitably there will be occasions when it's not possible to give the customer exactly what they want. Staying with the retail example, I might think that my local general store should carry printer cartridges for my printer to save me from having problems when the toner runs out. The trouble is, I only buy a cartridge about twice a year, probably no one else around has the same printer, and chances are I'll change printer before I've bought more than a handful of cartridges. It doesn't make commercial sense, and I'd be happy to be told that (in the right way). By the same token, if, like many other parents, I'm always running out of snacks for my children to take to school, it wouldn't do the local shop any harm to respond to my request to provide them.

Whether or not you accede to your customers' requests, the simple act of asking them, then doing something about it (even if it's saying 'no' with a good reason) draws the business more into the customers' ownership. It's not enough just to ask them. Companies who ask you what you want then turn a deaf ear to any replies are just paying lip service to the concept, and will get the negative results they deserve.

A special case of this mechanism is when a customer offers an opinion unsolicited. These opportunities should be treated like gold dust. They have already taken one step towards mental ownership of your business – they think it is worth helping you. I'm not talking about angry responses to problems here, but positive suggestions for improvement. Most businesses get them occasionally, and most of them fail miserably to react in the right way.

To test this assertion, I wrote to the manager of a local supermarket. Totally unsolicited, I sent him a three-page report with suggestions for improvements to his supermarket's restaurant that would improve customer service. If the manager had charisma in mind, he should have responded dramatically. At the very least, he should have rung me personally within a day or two of getting the report. It would probably have made sense also to have asked me to go in for a chat, and certainly to write to me after (say) a month, detailing any changes that had been put in place in response to my suggestions. I would also throw in a bunch of vouchers to spend in the supermarket. If even one of those ideas were

HORROR STORY

SUPERMARKET UPDATE

'Eventually, around two weeks after sending the report, I received a letter from the supermarket manager. Sadly, as expected, it was the usual, bland, empty remarks.

'"Rest assured I have taken all the comments you raised on board and will endeavour to make all future visits to our restaurant satisfactory. We try to ensure all our customers receive first-class customer service and facilities, however it is clear that on recent occasions we have failed to reach this objective and I apologize for that. Your feedback will certainly help us achieve our goal and if I can be of any further assistance to you please do not hesitate to contact me at the store."

'It's not all bad. He has apologized, rather than try to make excuses. He does appear to take the comments on board. But there are still two crucial failures. It took too long to reply, and there is nothing specific in the letter. As a customer I have no idea whether he took any notice of my report, or dropped it sniggering into the bin. I have no idea when and how things will get better. And to add insult to injury, he couldn't even be bothered to sign the letter. Finally, over a month after receiving the letter nothing has happened in the restaurant. If this is typical of this particular supermarket chain, they are in real trouble.'

worthwhile, the marginal value of vouchers for (say) a week's shopping would be trivially covered by the value of the suggestion.

So what did the manager do? Ten days on from sending the report, nothing. No response at all. If I do get anything, I'll bet that it's a standard 'thank you for your suggestions, we will give them serious consideration' screed, churned out from the mail merge. It's crass. It's madness. Not only is he overlooking some effective suggestions (I'd normally charge a significant amount for a report like that), by not responding he is irritating a customer. What would a telephone call have cost him? Five minutes of his time and a local call. What could he lose by his apparent distaste? A lifetime's food shopping for a family of four – £100,000 or more. That's an expensive phone call.

Let's imagine the events inside the supermarket when the letter and report arrived. The manager opens it. He shakes his head. Would you believe it? Some idiot thinks he knows how to run his restaurant better the management does. Hasn't he got enough problems without cranks trying to interfere? The writer is probably just touting for business. At this stage he either bins the letter or passes it to the restaurant manager with a note saying, 'What do you think of this?' The restaurant manager takes the suggestions as a personal criticism. And he bins it. After all, it's not his job to give customers what they want, is it?

PUTTING THEM IN CONTROL

As the last section suggests, a step towards the sense of ownership can be generated by as simple an action as listening to the customers and giving them what they ask for. Another basic step is to give the customer more control over the way things work. After all, whoever controls the business, owns the business. Sometimes control can be something that you wouldn't even think of in these terms.

❝Whoever controls the business, owns the business.❞

GOOD NEWS STORY

NOW WE'RE COOKING

'This restaurant in Columbus, Ohio, goes out of its way to ensure that customers are in control of their experience, even when it runs contrary to the way restaurants traditionally operate.

'This place is called Cookers. One of the things they do, the manager always stops buy and checks how it's going. On the food, on the service. If you don't like the food – not just if there's something wrong with it – they'll knock it off your bill.

'One of the great things is you don't have to have the same person wait on your table right through a meal. When we had a group in, we might get seven different people serving simultaneously. There was no having to find "your" waiter or waitress to pay. It didn't matter who you spoke to. In other places, and I know, I've worked in restaurants, it's run for the staff's benefit – they want to make sure of their tips, so no one else deals with their tables, even if the customers are in a hurry. That means if your server is busy you can wait a long time. In Cookers it is what the customers want that comes first.'

The self-service buffet is a wonderful example of subtle delegation of control. There's a boom in our town at the moment of restaurants offering fixed price, self-service buffet lunches. Everyone from Pizza Hut down to one-site Mexican and Italian watering holes are on the self-service buffet kick. What does it give the customer? As much as you can eat for a very reasonable price. And control. The customer decides what they will have and when they will eat it. They decide what they will put alongside what. Control of the meal has moved from the waiter and the chef into the hands of the customer.

> 66The self-service buffet is a wonderful example of subtle delegation at work.99

This is exactly the same benefit that the shopper in a self-service store has over a traditional store where you have to go and ask the guy behind the counter for what you want. There are times you want a friendly face – to ask for advice and recommendations – and self-service done well will always give you the opportunity to get that. I can't remember how many times I've been into DIY stores and there has been no one at the advice/information desk – that's just not good enough. But giving the customer control helps establish the feeling that, 'This is my business'.

Unfortunately, for retailers the practice of self-service is so widespread that there is no competitive advantage in it. For a supermarket to gain charisma out of giving more control you have to take delegation a step further, like Safeway's Shop and Go system (see page 57). But many other businesses do not give their customers the chance to take charge of the business process. There's an opportunity waiting there.

SPECIAL BENEFITS

If you own a business you expect to get something special out of it. Perhaps discounts, ability to get to stock out of hours and other benefits accruing from your ownership. In a reversal of this position, the more you can give your customers special benefits, the more ownership they will feel. We have already seen some benefits applied to shareholders. Such an approach can be widened to all regular shoppers, whether or not you have a share scheme.

This isn't the same as a loyalty card points scheme. There's a fair amount of evidence that these don't generate loyalty, neither do they encourage a sense of ownership. It's more a case of getting the special treatment you might expect as an owner – but being able to give that treatment to your whole customer base.

> 66 Many businesses do not give their customers the chance to take charge of the business process. There's an opportunity waiting there. 99

> 66 If you own a business you expect to get something special out of it. 99

A basic enough example is the matter of toilets. Anyone who has young children has been in the position where your child is suddenly desperate. There isn't time to go out and find somewhere. You are in a large store, so you ask if they have any facilities. No, they haven't. No matter that the staff must have some form of bathroom, as far as you are concerned they don't have anything, because you don't belong. It's not your store.

The same argument can be applied to almost any business. You can always find new ways to give special benefits to your customers. And there will always be challenges where a degree of flexibility can change your relationship with a customer forever. A customer is in the reception of your legal firm. 'Excuse me,' she says, 'before my meeting with Mr Johnson I need to copy this document and I didn't get a chance to do it. Is there a copy shop somewhere nearby I can use?' Very wrong answer: 'No,' and return to chewing gum, painting nails or reading magazine. Modestly wrong answer: 'Yes, just down the road on the left.' Right answer: 'Use our machine, it's just over there.' After all, if it's the customer's business, surely they can expect you to help them out?

MEET THE PEOPLE

When you own a company, it's often the case that you know some of the employees. The whole basis of the chapter titled 'They're people like us' was the component of charisma that comes from feeling that you know the staff as people – but there is a secondary impact that the better you know the staff, the more you own the business. In that chapter's terms, most of this will come from the front line staff. However, there's a subtle difference when you look at ownership.

An owner doesn't just deal with the front line people. It's the whole company. The best way to emphasize this is to get your senior management in face-to-face contact with the customers. Senior managers often feel that their task is purely strategic. That anything that takes them away from planning and

> 66 There will always be challenges where a degree of flexibility can change your relationship with a customer forever. 99

meetings and creative thinking about the future and negotiating mergers and takeovers is a distraction from the real work. But there's no point to all this magnificent strategy without the customers, and senior management who don't come into regular contact with the customers lose touch with the people at the coalface, and the very reason for the company's existence.

There has been a very popular series on UK television in which chief executives and chairmen of large companies go back to the real world, often working in customer contact jobs. It is fascinating that every time the executive learns a vast amount. The benefits to the company are immense. So much so that it's hard to understand why *every* chief executive, *every* senior manager doesn't spend a day each week on the front line. But there's an extra benefit that is relevant in this chapter. The more the customers come into practical contact with the people at the top, the more they will feel that they own the business.

Take the example of supermarkets. If I seem to be picking on supermarkets in this chapter it's just that they tend to feel very remote to the average customer. In most supermarkets you will occasionally see junior management, walking the store, looking at the produce and trying to avoid catching the eye of the customers. You will hardly ever see senior management at all – they are hidden away in the below-stairs warrens that most large stores have. It hardly makes you feel ownership. Yet supermarkets are in an ideal position to make contact with the person at the top easy.

Unless you are looking for a particular product, most shoppers don't really want to stop and talk to staff as they head around the store. However, there is one part of the journey where a conversation would be very welcome. In the checkout queues. Here are strings of people with nothing better to do. All customers. All with time on their hands. An ideal opportunity for senior

66 Senior management who don't come into regular contact with customers lose touch with the people at the coalface, and the very reason for the company's existence. 99

66 Supermarkets are in an ideal position to make contact with the person at the top easy. 99

managers to meet their customers, discuss the store, perhaps help them pack their shopping away and spread a sense of ownership. Yet I have never seen it done. The sense of ownership is very much in management hands. Here's a chance to do something about it.

DOING IT THEIR WAY

Whatever the vehicle you choose (or combination – you don't have to stick to a single route), your aim should be to give the customer the feeling of having you as his or her own personal company. Imagine yourself in the place of one of your customers for a moment. Think about the sorts of products and services he or she gets from you. Or could get from a competitor. Now imagine that you, the customer, own a company dedicated to your needs. Everything they do is specifically designed to meet your requirements. They are entirely yours. Compare that imaginary company to your own. That's the gap you have to bridge.

This doesn't mean you have to become that imaginary company. In most cases it would bankrupt you, and it's all very well to be one customer's imaginary company, but in reality you have to be the company each of your customers wants. This can lead to impossible conflicts. However, there isn't a company in existence that couldn't move further towards that imaginary company. Far enough so that most of your customers, or your most important customers, or even all of your customers can feel that you are *their* company.

> 66Your aim should be to give the customer the feeling of having you as his or her own personal company.99

10 CUTE AND CUDDLY

If technical wizardry appeals to our male character, this component appeals to the female. It can apply to the company as a whole, to products or to staff, but the aim is for the customers to have a protective approach to our company. This doesn't imply that the company is weak – we are looking for the sort of reaction a tiger cub would get.

HUG APPEAL

Cute and cuddly are very marketable properties. If it's possible to give your company or some aspect of it a cute and cuddly feel, there is a big opportunity for customer appeal. It might be as a result of imagery, or a very real feeling about your staff. Here again, it's often a small company approach that is the target. You can imagine a conversation between two friends. 'I've got this sweet little man who is the only person I would allow to service my boiler.' Condescending? Well, yes. Cute and cuddly isn't always the most enjoyable aspect of charisma to be on the receiving end of, but it's still a powerful ally in winning over some customers.

Of all the charisma components, this is probably the hardest to define clearly. We all know whether something is (and isn't) loveable, but it's very hard to give

“Cute and cuddly are very marketable properties.”

clear manufacturing specifications, unless your target audience is five year olds. The need is to evoke an emotion in the customer that combines delight and protectiveness. It's a watered-down version of the feeling of a parent for a child. Not easy to achieve – but it has been done, and can be done again.

THE MASCOT

One of the easier ways to invoke this component is to take an indirect approach. There might not be anything loveable about your company, there might not be anything cute about your products, but getting the company associated with something cuddly in the eyes of the public can give a subtle aura to the company as a whole. One of the best examples of how much the company does not have to be cuddly to employ this technique was the long-running tiger campaign from UK Exxon subsidiary Esso.

The use of a tiger is very clever in this respect. Because the emotions that are being used here contain a strong degree of protectiveness, there is inevitably an element of weakness in the picture. A baby may be loveable, but it is also frail. By using a tiger, the power of the animal negates any suggestion of frailty. In fact, the early images were all about power – 'Put a tiger in your tank' implied that using this fuel would pep up your car. But there was more to it than that.

Tigers may be powerful, but they are also extremely beautiful. And tiger cubs have plenty of 'aww' factor. The play for the cuddly image soon followed. There was a craze for a year or two of having 'tiger tail' fluffy imitation fur tails tied to radio aerials. Advertising made more use of tiger images. As technical sophistication increased, the move to dramatic live action shots of tigers may have stressed the power aspect of the beast – but there was still always the combination of beauty and a deadly cuddliness. Tigers may not have won over everyone to Esso, but there's no doubt they did a lot for the company's image.

Another long-running UK advertising campaign for Andrex toilet rolls features puppies. Here the cuteness is full-frontal. There is no suggestion of anything but

66Getting the company associated with something cuddly in the eyes of the public can give a subtle aura to the company as a whole.99

cuddliness. The puppies are allegedly used to emphasize how soft yet strong the product is, but there's no doubt at all that this is a straightforward attempt to associate a product and brand with the cute nature of the mascot – and it works.

There's a fine line between the use of beauty and the bringing in of sexual allure in selling. Despite the nominal politically correct views about not using people as sex objects, manufacturers of everything from perfume to cars use attractive actors of both sexes to put their point across. Again these are, in effect, mascots for the company and the product, there to win your affection and transfer it to the sale.

A LOVEABLE COMPANY

Because this diffuse property is one we tend to apply to individual humans and creatures, it is particularly difficult to apply to a company. Usually a company is a non-concrete concept. We relate to the staff, to the products, to the environment – but it is hard to think of the company as cuddly. What do you think of when you envisage a company? The logo, the premises, attributes of the products and services – but it's usually hard to get a grip on the company itself.

The key factor seems to be the way attributes are usually applied to the people or the location or the products. To make the company itself loveable, you have to get the attributes linked directly to it. A classic example of getting it right is Anita Roddick's Body Shop. You might have opinions about the shops or the products (I find the smell of the shops positively stomach-churning), but the company itself is hung about with an ethos of caring. Caring for the third world, for the environment, for animals. All good things. All things you can adopt cynically, jumping on the bandwagon, but somehow you get the impression that with Anita Roddick it's for real.

66Here the cuteness is full-frontal.99

66The key factor seems to be the way attributes are usually applied to the people or the location or the products. To make the company itself loveable, you have to get the attributes linked directly to it.99

Compare the way that the Body Shop has done this, with the way a typical corporate approaches its environmental image. Many large companies sponsor the arts or sport. Many large companies spend money on the environment. And you'll see their logo wherever they are involved. The Body Shop inverts the approach. Instead of seeing the Body Shop getting free advertising elsewhere you will see the environmental message on Body Shop bags. You will see third world concern in its window displays and in Anita Roddick's appearances on the TV (remember the star at the top from earlier?).

Time and again, the Body Shop takes the time to put across its caring image. The brown paper bags. The recycled bottles for perfume. You can't shop at the Body Shop and not be aware that it's a company that cares. And caring is a loveable quality. If you really intend to give your company a specific image, you have to go out of your way to do it. Token gestures aren't enough, you have to go over the top and keep going over the top. You can make a company loveable – by your words and your actions – but only if the characteristic is central to the way you operate.

PRODUCTS THAT SAY 'HOLD ME'

Sometimes there is something about a product that just makes you want to hold it, almost to caress it. It could be something that is literally cuddly, like a soft toy. A great example is Ty's assorted Beanie ranges. By hitting the dual buttons of collectability and cuddliness, Ty has produced a worldwide market far beyond anything you might expect from collectors alone. You just can't imagine the same attraction from collecting matchboxes or plastic model fruit. The cuddliness counts. Equally, though, it can be a more sophisticated attraction.

I have a wooden box. It is hand-made, by a craftsman who takes a piece of wood and makes a box that suits the wood. It's not a regular shape – it's almost like a tree stump, but the surface is beautifully smooth. Functionally, as a pure

66Caring is a loveable quality.**99**

66You can make a company loveable but only if the
characteristic is central to the way you operate.**99**

box, it is nothing special. It can hold a few cuff links or some small change. But it just feels so good to touch. It is enjoyable to hold. Just popping the lid on feels right.

What gives the box its feel? There's a combination of elements. The natural material. The organic shape. The smooth curves. The perfect fit of the lid. Remember again the source of this particular component of charisma. It is based on a natural affection. And that seems to make it easier to apply to natural products. The wood, the smooth, flowing yet irregular shape, all combine to make the box feel as much grown as manufactured. The fact that it is made by a single, identifiable human being rather than a faceless production line helps give the box its loveable touch.

These elements won't work for every company. It might not be appropriate to use natural materials; it may not work to have an individual crafted product or a unique shape. But it certainly could apply to many more companies than it does at the moment. Note, by the way, that you should not make the popular mistake of assuming that anything natural is acceptable. Just as the health food fanatics who only eat natural additives are opening themselves up in theory to exposure to belladonna, heroin and alkaloid poisons, having a natural product is not enough on its own. Petroleum is natural. Excrement is natural. You need a product that carries the appealing, almost the sanitized side of nature.

THE NOSTALGIA FACTOR

There is a special case of cute and cuddly that is based in nostalgia. It's the misty-eyed remembrance of the way things were – or at least they way we like to imagine things were – in a simpler, cosier past. This is a great vehicle for charisma, provided you really deliver. Too many products aimed at the nostalgia market are just the same as the ordinary products on the shelf, but with nostalgia packaging. This can lead to disappointment. But it is quite possible to harness the nostalgia factor more effectively.

❝You need a product that carries the appealing, almost the sanitized side of nature.❞

GOOD NEWS STORY

BEETLE BEAUTY

When the new Volkswagen Beetle was sold in the USA, each car had a cut-glass vase on the dash, holding a flower. Evoking the classic days of motoring, this simple gift set the tone for the relationship between customer and dealer – it was a touch of brilliance.

A good example is the use of steam trains. These majestic machines, almost universally loved by adults and children alike, are now reappearing increasingly, either working small private railroads or pulling special trains on the ordinary track. If your company has a product that can benefit from the nostalgia factor, what better way to get this across than to have a tie-in with steam. Sell the products on a steam train; have a train tour the country carrying your name and message. The options are as varied as your imagination can make them.

If it fits your image, the nostalgia factor can be used everywhere. We explore it on page 197 with reference to the tills in shops. Some companies use recreated period vehicles to provide their deliveries. Others provide vacation bus services in rebuilt vintage vehicles. Just make sure, if you want to make the nostalgia charismatic, that you follow through. Really make your 'granny's recipe' biscuits with an old-fashioned remedy. Make a big thing of no added colouring and preservatives – it not only emphasizes the reality of the nostalgia,

66 The options are as varied as your imagination can make them. 99

66 If it fits your image, the nostalgia factor can be used everywhere. 99

66 Just make sure, if you want to make the nostalgia charismatic, that you follow through. 99

but hits a whole new healthy eating market that wants to avoid such things. Use nostalgia, but give it depth.

STAFF TO DIE FOR

How about the staff themselves? Can't they be cute and loveable? Yes, to a point, but again this is a difficult one to pitch. Everyone might be friendly and loveable at a theme park, but there's always that nagging feeling that the smile is painted on and they hate you underneath. By all means have staff that are cute and loveable if they are appropriate to your business – cute and loveable may not give the right message if it is important to convey to your customers that you are serious, high flyers – but make sure that you recruit for it rather than trying to impose a uniform plastic cuteness.

Exactly what you recruit for in trying to get loveable front line staff is interesting. A while ago, when I was managing a large PC group for a corporate, I held interviews for a job. One of the applicants was a stunningly attractive woman. After the interview, the uniform response from my staff, male and female, was, 'Well, she's got the job, hasn't she?' As it happened she didn't, because other applicants had much more appropriate experience. To have a recruitment policy that puts attractiveness to the opposite sex at the top of the priority list would be to miss the point entirely. Your customers might be unable to take their eyes off this person, but it wouldn't take much dealing with an icy personality to put them off.

When dealing with customer contact staff, cute and cuddly has to be primarily about personality. Someone who is bright, bubbly, personable – all the adjectives that suggest that having a conversation with them will be an absolute delight. If they are also good looking it's a bonus. I know in a politically correct world we shouldn't distinguish between people on looks, but the fact is we do.

66 Use nostalgia, but give it depth. 99

66 When dealing with customer contact staff, cute and cuddly has to be primarily about personality. 99

Everyone does, including customers. The right sort of looks will certainly complement the right personality – but they aren't enough alone. For that matter, the right sort of looks doesn't necessarily mean the characteristics that are expected in a catwalk model or of a film star. Maybe the looks of an attractive boy or girl next door would feel safer.

COMPANY AT RISK

Part of the appeal of cute little lambs or human babies is their vulnerability. In some ways it can be advantageous for your company to be the underdog. Perhaps not as absolutely at risk as this section title suggests, but finding a way that makes customers want to protect your company increases their sense of ownership and increases your inherent cuddliness.

This underdog position is one that can be milked to great effect if your company is large but not the biggest player in your market. A classic example of this would be the Avis campaign that turned the car hire company around. After struggling to deflect attention from its position as number 2 in the car hire business, Avis realized that there would be much more benefit from emphasizing it. The message that because Avis was number 2 they had to try harder really hit home. The customers liked dealing with a company that hadn't got big-headed enough to think that it was the biggest there was, and hence the best.

When you are under competitive attack from a bigger company, remember this. You may feel outgunned, but you have a real advantage. Although consumers want the nominal stability of buying from a very big company, they don't actually like big companies. They prefer smaller businesses. So even if you are an enormous multi-national giant, if you're a smaller player in a particular

66 In some ways it can be advantageous for your company to be the underdog. 99

66 Although consumers want the nominal stability of buying from a very big company, they don't actually like big companies. 99

market you can emphasize that position to bring out all the benefits of smallness, and to win the sympathy vote.

BEING CUTE

As I have emphasized several times in this chapter, this is the hardest of the components to do anything with. Some aspects of it simply won't work with a fair number of companies. Others require careful selection of staff or a devotion to a message that your shareholders or stakeholders don't see as key to your business. Yet that doesn't mean that this component should be ignored. It has worked very effectively in some companies. It is worth exploring for yours.

11

WE KEEP IN TOUCH

Relationships are made or broken by the quality of communication. Having a real, lifetime dialogue with the customer and using all means available – especially now that new electronic channels have wider penetration – is an essential.

KEEPING UP THE DIALOGUE

Dialogue is the oil of human relations. Not just communications, but two-way communications. Talking and listening. Arguably the most powerful and yet the simplest component of charisma is getting your communications right. Simplest, at least in understanding its value, but you only have to watch a news bulletin to realize just how bad we human beings are at the business of communication.

Compared to the animals we have uniquely sophisticated languages. The technology of communication has evolved to the extent that it's possible to have a normal telephone conversation with someone at the South Pole. The Internet has opened the same flexible worldwide communication to documents that the telephone did to the spoken word. And yet news story after news story is about failed peace talks, about failures in communication between individuals or companies or countries.

66 **Dialogue is the oil of human relations.** 99

From the customer's viewpoint, poor communications can wreck a perfectly acceptable delivery of service. You might think that you have done your job if a product that a customer ordered was delivered on time. Yet if you failed to respond to a query about the order, this failure would far outweigh the fact that you had made the delivery. In fact, while no customer will tolerate repeatedly poor service delivery, it is certainly often the case for an individual occurrence that it is better to fail on delivery but keep up good communication on what is happening than it is to deliver with no communication at all. It's that important.

WE LISTEN

Listening to the customer is a good starting point. When customers call you up, you should be really interested, whatever they are saying. These are the people who pay your wages and keep your company in business. They are inherently interesting. Remember my letter and report sent to a supermarket manager (see page 151). That should have made fascinating reading. He should have listened to my comments, or at least read them. Perhaps he did. I don't know, because his reply was so vague that it could have been a standard, off-the-shelf complaints letter. It's not enough to listen to customers, you have to be seen to listen.

This all sounds painfully time consuming. In the supermarket I mentioned, the guy was running a busy store. He had lots to do, rather than listen to an individual customer. But bear in mind, as always, lifetime value. That £100,000 or more that he is risking by not taking a moment to let me know that he had listened. That sounds worth a few minutes of anyone's time.

❝From the customer's viewpoint, poor communication can wreck a perfectly acceptable delivery of service.❞

❝It's not enough to listen to customers, you have to be seen to listen.❞

HORROR STORY

WE LISTEN, BUT WE DON'T HEAR

The supplier of this story was trying to fix a mortgage. He needed it quickly, or he would lose the house he had set his heart on purchasing. To get the mortgage he needed to have a letter from his solicitor registered by the building society (savings and loan).

'The letter was sent by my solicitor. A week later I phoned the building society. The letter had not been received. So I phoned the solicitor – the letter had been sent. I phoned the building society and they said they would re-enquire.

'A week later I phoned the building society – they enquired and were assured that the letter had been sent by the solicitor but not been received. I phoned the solicitor; he confirmed that the letter has been sent.

'Another week later I phoned the building society – no letter had been received, and they would make enquiries. This cycle continued until I happened to speak to the same person on the call answering team. The cycle emerged slowly. The building society would call the solicitor to ask if a letter had been sent, the answer was yes so no further action was taken. There was no system in place to ensure that something was done if the letter was not received! The solicitor's office just kept saying they had sent the letter.

'The complication was that there were three teams in the building society – call answering, decision making and call back (to me). As the whole picture was not in the possession of any of them, there was no way they could tell that nothing was happening. Actions to follow up were lost in the system as their computer was crashing and restoring back-up files. So despite reassurances that things were registered in the system when I would phone the next day (this got to be daily) the system no longer held the information put on the previous day!'

❝Being seen to listen is just the first stage.❞

Being seen to listen is just the first stage. Listening is fine. But just listening and nodding (being seen to listen) doesn't make a relationship. It's like talking to an analyst – it's not like dealing with a friend, because it is all listening. To really reinforce the benefit of listening you need to let the customer know just what you have done as a result of what you heard.

Take my report to the supermarket manager on improving his restaurant. An early section of the report detailed minor fixes that were essential if he were to drag the restaurant out of the low-esteem position it had reached. They included basics like replacing the missing seat tops of two stools at a bar-style table, and making sure that there was always an ample supply of napkins. These were actions the manager was almost bound to take at some point if he were to keep the restaurant viable. Think how much better I, a customer, would feel if he had written back, thanked me for the report and told me that he would be implementing these recommendations immediately. Not only would he have listened, he would have done something.

Now the manager may well have been intending to make these changes anyway. He may well have made them saying, 'I'll do this despite the idiot who dared send me a report on how to improve my restaurant.' But if he had communicated to me that the changes were as a result of my observations I couldn't help but feel pleased. At least for a little while.

Then I would realize that he had not told me about anything else. The communication had dried up. And the doubts would start to come in. What about all my other recommendations? What had he thought of them? A sensible response campaign for this case would probably involve several communications. A telephone call within a day or two of receiving the report. A letter a few days later, identifying the easy actions that are to be taken right away and saying he would get back to me by a certain date on the rest of the report.

It may happen that during the next week a real crisis blows up. There isn't time to respond to the other recommendations. The easy answer is just to

❝To really reinforce the benefit of listening you need to let the customer know just what you have done as a result of what you heard.❞

ignore it for the moment. A few days here or there won't make much difference. Except an expectation has been set up. I expect a communication from the manager by a certain date, and when it doesn't happen I feel let down. If there isn't time to do the real thing, at least make the time to send a note, or even better make a phone call to say sorry, you've been held up, but you'll have something by a new date. That call makes all the difference.

The next communication may be a mixed message. Some suggestions will be taken up. Others will be impractical. It would include details of why they were impractical and emphasize that the supermarket is always open to suggestions and is really thankful for the effort. It would probably be sensible throw in some vouchers for use in the store at this point, as it's a natural break in communication. But not the end. A month or two later I would make one last phone call to check with the customer that everything was okay with the changes made at the customer's suggestion. Over the top? Too much communication? Not at all, just making sure that the dialogue contained effective listening – and that the customer knew that listening and action were taking place.

GOOD NEWS STORY

REMOTE LISTENING

All too often we don't actually hear what the customer says. We know we're right. This hotel really listens.

'I stayed at the Mina Seyahi hotel in Dubai, and left my phone there when I left the country. I called the hotel, who put me through to housekeeping. They said they hadn't found the phone, but took my number (back home) in case it turned up.

'I then called them back and asked them to look under the bed. They phoned back quickly to say they had found the phone. I asked them to send it by courier, and the phone arrived within two days.'

66Giving customers a steady flow of information is essential to maintain a relationship.99

WE TALK

Just as letting your customers know what is happening as a result of a complaint or a suggestion is an important part of listening, giving customers a steady flow of information is essential to maintain a relationship. Keeping the customer aware of what is happening is just as important part way through a long-term contract as it is when responding immediately to a customer suggestion. As soon as the customer is uncertain about progress they become uncomfortable about their relationship with you and any possibility of charisma disappears.

In this age of information overload it might seem strange to seem to be asking you to bombard your customer with communications – but this isn't really the case. Much information overload comes from unnecessary and unwanted communication. Junk e-mail. The memo writer who feels he has to copy his words of wisdom to everyone in the company, just in case, to guard his back. Most of the time we are very happy to receive information from our friends, or about something we are interested in. We certainly like to get information that reduces uncertainty and stress.

The more your company is like a friend to the customer, the more they will appreciate your communications. And they will certainly do so when engaged in business with you. Whether or not they are explicitly agreed, we all have mental milestones when a project of any sort is underway. If we get well past a milestone and haven't heard that everything has been done that we expect by that point, we get uncomfortable. If you are to make communication with your customers work, you need to establish what their milestones are, and make sure that you communicate at those points. It might seem a lot of effort, but with an

66Much information overload comes from unnecessary and unwanted communication.99

HORROR STORY

WHAT DO YOU MEAN, TALK?

'Flying from India, we flew Benares to Delhi to Amman to London. We were told by Royal Jordanian that we had to check in three hours prior to departure. I pointed out that this was 3:30 am and there'd be no one there. They said that if we weren't there three hours before they couldn't guarantee a seat. Naturally there was no one at the desk until something approaching 5:00 am.

'The flight was then delayed by fog. The PA system was useless as it couldn't be heard anywhere in the departure lounge. Eventually, having heard nothing from Royal Jordanian (every other airline had a representative in the lounge) I managed to blag my way through passport control and got to their office. They told me that there was a nine-hour delay. I said they needed to tell everyone that. They said that they'd made lots of announcements. I said that the PA system couldn't be heard in the lounge and he said, "Yes, it's awful isn't it?" At this point I got annoyed and suggested that he might like to put an airline representative in the lounge. He said of course he would and then did nothing about it for the remainder of the delay. I went back through passport control four times to get updates that I relayed to other RJ passengers.

'We missed our onward connection in Amman. By the time we got home the delay was 25 hours. Not once did anyone from RJ say sorry. At one point when a woman was losing her temper in Amman one of the staff said, "We've fed you, we're putting you into a hotel, we've arranged onward travel for you, what more do you want?" Naturally her reply wasn't repeatable.'

electronic diary or contact management system it is trivial to schedule contacts in this way – and well worth it to keep the customer happy.

Exactly how frequent those milestones are depends on the customer and on the project. It may be necessary to report progress each week, or even each day.

> 66The more your company is like a friend to the customer, the more they will appreciate your communications.99

Or it may be enough to say, 'We don't expect anything to happen for the next six months. We'll give you an update then, even if nothing has happened still.' And, of course, keep to that promise. It doesn't have to be about something big. The whole exercise could be about delivering a leaflet, as in our next story.

HORROR STORY

WHAT COMMUNICATION?

'Some time ago Cable & Wireless leafleted my area, saying that they could now offer phone and TV services in here. The leaflet was full of promotional puff and nice graphics, but didn't actually give any information as to what services they offered, prices etc. So I phoned the number given to get some more information (with the full intention to swap from my current company if it seemed like a good deal). After listening to hold music for ten minutes (a phone company which doesn't answer the phone!), I got through to a woman who couldn't give me any price or service information, but said that there was another leaflet which listed them. But she couldn't send me the leaflet because they had run out and wouldn't be back in stock for another three weeks. I gave her my address but never received anything. Unsurprisingly I have no intention to ever use their services!

'Of course this is an example of C&W's poor planning, organization and internal communication, which resulted in their marketing department trying to sell a product that the organization couldn't deliver. It must have been pretty disheartening for the customer service staff too.'

Exactly how you choose to communicate will depend on your circumstances and the value of the customer, but bear in mind that there is a hierarchy of communication values. The more personal, the more physical the communication, the higher the value to the recipient. Generally you can't beat face-to-

❝Exactly how you choose to communicate will depend on your circumstances and the value of the customer, but bear in mind that there is a hierarchy of communication values.❞

face communication, while impersonal mass e-mailings probably come near the bottom of the hierarchy. Two factors conspire against this natural hierarchy applying in all cases, however.

There are times when the written word is more powerful than the spoken, even face-to-face. If you want most impact on the individual customer, yes, go for face-to-face. But if your customer will get more benefit out of showing others your communication, then having it in a written form is more beneficial. You might find, for instance, that a supplier would rather have a written pat on the back that they can copy to other potential customers than a verbal one that gives them more of a personal lift.

There is also an oddity of e-mail that often brings it significantly higher up the communication hierarchy than many would lead you to believe. An e-mail may be one of the least powerful means of communication, but it has one huge benefit over writing letters or face-to-face conversations – it is extremely easy to do. It is so much easier to send off an e-mail than to write and post a letter, for instance. And an e-mail that gets sent will always score better on the communication value scale than the most beautiful hand-written letter that remains in the writer's mind and never makes it into the post.

BREAKING DOWN THE BARRIERS

Most businesses are littered with barriers to communication. It seems that we might love our customers – but only at a distance. When we risk face-to-face communication it is only with the sorts of protection in place that you might expect in a high-security prison. I have already mentioned the screens that separate railway station staff and their customers (see page 58). These present terrible barriers to communication. You can't hear properly. You can't see very

66An e-mail may be one of the least powerful means of communication, but... it is extremely easy to do.99

66It seems that we might love our customers – but only a distance.99

well. The staff member is distanced and remote. Any transfer of money or tickets has to be done through a little trapdoor. You could never have proper face-to-face communication this way. Yet does a railway station selling tickets need this sort of security, when banks can now get away with open tills and super-fast shutters? What is it that is so dangerous about selling railway tickets compared with selling plane tickets, for instance, usually done at an open, unprotected desk?

In fact, it's arguable that much of the customer anger that the railway barriers are presumably there to defend against comes from the inability to communicate effectively. The fact remains that if banks can avoid putting physical barriers in the way of interpersonal communications, and can avoid treating all customers as potential criminals, then so can every other company that is dealing with customers face-to-face. It is very sad that a small number of people attack practically anyone giving them service – even medical staff in hospitals – but to turn everywhere into outward-facing prisons because of this is not the right reaction. By all means protect against criminals, but not at the expense of the rest of us.

Barriers aren't always the visible ones of bullet-proof glass and iron bars. Barriers come in all forms. They might be time dependent. A company that only provides service during office hours is putting up a time-based barrier. Alternatively, the barrier might be to different means of communication. I have seen companies strongly discouraging the use of letters. They point out that they can deal with problems more quickly on the phone. They don't bother to point out that using letters means that the customer has an audit trail of their dialogue. While most e-companies and high-technology companies list e-mail addresses for customer service, surprisingly few others do. Check your utility bills.

> 66 Much... customer anger... comes from the inability to communicate effectively. 99

> 66 By all means protect against criminals, but not at the expense of the rest of us. 99

HORROR STORY

PAYING FOR THE PRIVILEGE TO BUY

'I bought a video from Dixon's and after about six months it broke. My service agreement had said they would collect it but apparently there was some kind of loophole meaning I had to take it to my nearest Dixon's. Their customer services assured me that the shop was open till 6 so I dashed home from work, grabbed the video and walked for about two miles to get to the shop. I arrived at 5.45. It was shut.

'Two weeks later I was burgled. One of the items stolen was a stereo made by Dixon's. For insurance purposes, I needed a quote from Dixon's to replace it. It belonged to my flatmate so I wasn't personally going to buy a new one. Dixon's wanted to charge me £10 to give me a quote scribbled on a compliments slip. I explained that as it had been a Dixon's own make obviously it would be replaced by purchasing a new one from Dixons and did they really feel it necessary to charge me – they did.

'About a month later I was running a promotion through work and wanted to give away some electronic organizers (about 100 in total). I went to my local Dixon's near work and asked if they could quote for supplying and what discount they would offer. They informed me that I could pay £10 for a quote but I wouldn't get any discount for a bulk purchase.

'Now thoroughly pissed off (!) I wrote to Dixon's head office. I calculated that by annoying me so much they had forfeited about £3,000. I wrote a letter of complaint. That was six years ago. I never got a reply.'

❝E-mail provides a great new way to keep the communication flowing with your customers.❞

There may be perfectly acceptable reasons for applying a particular limitation. It may be that providing customer service during office hours is all that is economically viable using conventional means. But that doesn't mean that you shouldn't look for ways around the limitations. Even if it is something as simple as voicemail, e-mail and a Web site. The fact is, the fewer obstructions you put in the way of communications from your customer, the better the chance of having a good dialogue and building up a positive relationship. Consider every possible channel of communication at every time of day. What is possible? What is your response time like? You may be happy with the outcome – but make sure your customers are too.

The Dixon's story is a remarkable demonstration of actively setting up barriers. Overlooking the bad timing, the two examples of charging for a quote are bizarre. It is almost as if the company were going out of its way to avoid getting business. This is particularly well demonstrated in the second example. A business customer with an order for 100 units, from a large, respectable company that may well want more orders in the future – and the reaction was to charge for a quote and refuse a discount. The salespeople should have been round to the customer's office with discounts in hand! And then to top it all, no letter of reply. It's a very sad case.

HITTING THE E-MAIL

E-mail provides a great new way to keep the communication flowing with your customers. At first sight e-mail is just a crippled version of the conventional mail. After all, there are still a good many of your customers who don't have access to e-mail. But this is a fatally limiting view of a medium that went from practically nothing to an everyday part of life in a handful of years. Compared, for instance, to the telephone, e-mail's speed of penetration into the customer base has been phenomenal.

66 Compared to the telephone, e-mail's speed of penetration into the customer base has been phenomenal. 99

Right from the start it was obvious that there was something special about e-mail. When the Internet's predecessor, the Arpanet, was set up, it was designed to overcome a very specific problem. When an individual wanted to use different computers they had to do so via a separate terminal connected to each. The Arpanet made it possible to switch a terminal between computers. But it also provided for computer-to-computer traffic. Someone who was playing around with the possibilities of the technology cobbled together a system that allowed users to send each other messages, from university to university, across the USA. Within a couple of years, e-mail traffic was dominating the Arpanet. That was in the 1970s. By the 1990s most large businesses had internal e-mail, but it was only with the commercial opening up of the Internet in the latter half of the 1990s that e-mail really flew.

But why? Why is it so popular? Let's start with simple nuts-and-bolts messaging. Just sending a piece of text. Why is a text e-mail any better than writing a letter? For all its critics, claiming that e-mail has ruined letter writing, the benefits are immense:

- *Immediacy.* You send off an e-mail, and it can be anywhere in the world in seconds. It has the speed of using the telephone with neither the cost nor the need for the recipient to be waiting for it at the other end.

- *Duplication.* One e-mail can be sent to ten people with the same ease as it can be sent to one.

- *Cheapness.* No other text communication can compare for cheapness.

- *Low effort.* Ignoring typing the text, it takes me seconds to send an e-mail, without ever leaving my desk. To send something in the post I have to put it in an envelope, address the envelope, obtain and attach a stamp (checking the weight for the postage) and get the letter to the post box.

- *Easy addressing.* It is often much easier to find or to guess an e-mail address than a postal address.

The flexibility of e-mail has a secondary but important implication. Because it is so easy to send off an e-mail, it's possible to send a note straight away and get rid of a nagging task that might otherwise be at the back of your mind, clogging up mental resources for hours or days. An e-mail gets a task ticked off in your mental list instantly.

These advantages don't come entirely free. The low effort means that it is all too easy to send an e-mail without really thinking about the content. This results not only in bad spelling and grammar, but in messages that really shouldn't have been sent if only a moment's thought had been applied. The cheapness and ease of duplication mean that a lot of mails are sent to people who never really wanted them. Whether we are dealing with junk e-mails or the corporate habit of copying in everyone who might possibly be interested, this profligacy means that e-mails add to information overload.

Neither of these is a total disaster. It is quite possible to develop a habit of rereading an e-mail before sending it. With careful use, the ability to send cheaply and widely is still a real benefit – as in all other communications, focus is important. The immediacy results in a rather different problem. Because e-mails get to their destination so quickly they occupy a psychological position between a phone call and a letter. Though we don't expect quite as quick a response as with a phone call, we certainly expect to get a reply to an e-mail much quicker than a letter. Anything over a couple of days and we feel that we are being kept waiting.

Ideally, an e-mail should be answered within 24 hours, unless it is a purely social message in which case the rapid-fire response can be overwhelming. This is an important consideration when using e-mail to communicate with your customers. Offering an e-mail address is an essential, but it's not enough. You also have to respond quickly.

❝An e-mail gets a task ticked off your mental list instantly.❞

❝As in all other communications, focus is important.❞

❝Offering an e-mail address is an essential, but it's not enough. You also have to respond quickly.❞

E-mail technology can be some help in this respect. Most commercial e-mail systems provide auto-responders that allow a generic 'we've got your mail' message to be sent out immediately on receipt of incoming mail to a particular address. The decision whether or not to use an auto-responder is a delicate balance. After all, it doesn't actually give the customers what they have asked for and will add to their inbox overload. Even so, it is probably worthwhile as long as it is handled the right way. A good auto-responder mail will reassure the customer that their mail has been received (a real benefit with a black hole communication system like e-mail) and should give them accurate information of when they will get a response.

This timing part is essential. You should be specific – 'We will respond in two working days' rather than 'We will get back you as soon as possible.' If for any reason that two-day deadline has to be breached, the customer should get an explanatory (and apologetic) mail detailing when they will now get a response. It is tempting to put advertising into a mail like this. After all, it is reaching a targeted group. Resist the temptation. If a customer is contacting you, they probably aren't asking to be sold to – don't force it on them in an e-mail that isn't actually delivering what they asked for.

In making such a communication, give them alternative routes in case they can't wait for your reply. Refer them to the Web site, phone numbers, physical locations. Keep the language positive without being smug and overbearing. And don't try to pretend that the mail is from a real person. It is obviously automatic, so it is probably best to make it from a team rather than an individual.

When the real reply is written, it's a different matter. The ease of duplication of e-mail makes it particularly tempting to use stock replies. There's nothing wrong with having templates and stock phrases – but make sure that the specific e-mail is appropriate for the individual. This mail should be signed by an individual – not the chief executive or another figurehead, but the person who is handling this customer. And include a personal return e-mail address for that individual, not a generic address.

❝Make sure that the specific e-mail is appropriate for the individual.❞

We could stop now and still consider e-mails to be a superb vehicle for communication with those customers who have access to them, but it is possible to go further. E-mails might have started as pure text, but now they have the potential to be much more. You can format the contents like a Web page. You can include graphics. You can attach documents and files. E-mails have gone from being plain memos to an envelope you can stuff with appropriate content.

This is of real benefit in communication. Just being able to send a document this way, or to give your e-mail a more attractive format enhances your ability to communicate, providing a broader bandwidth and more flexibility. But with this power comes a degree of responsibility. It's fine to format your e-mails using the HTML language of the Web, provided your customer's mail programs can handle it. Give them the option of switching it on for future communications rather than assuming they can cope. And if you send them documents, make sure your virus checking is up to date and effective.

This second requirement may seen obvious, but in one year I have received Word documents containing viruses from both a Web search site and an airline. Not only was this careless, their response to my notifying them was appalling. The Web search site simply ignored my e-mails. The airline representative did bother to reply, but only to tell me that it was okay, because his PC had now been swept clean of viruses. He seemed blithely uncaring of the fact that he had infected several customers' PCs, not bothering even to apologize.

The fact remains that e-mails have a huge potential for improving customer communications (and hence charisma) if only companies took notice. The starting point is making a customer contact e-mail address well known and easy to remember. Getting customers to use this route will both save you money on answering their comments and open up a powerful new channel for proactive communication. The second essential is to deal with the e-mail in a timely fashion, suiting the timescales of e-mail rather than those of the post. And the third is to take notice – to actually do something. Don't just acknowledge the customer's e-mail, make something happen, and tell them about it.

❝The fact remains that e-mails have a huge potential for improving customer communication.❞

HORROR STORY

RELUCTANT WEB SITES

This customer has found that plenty of companies think that it is enough to publish an e-mail address without having the mechanisms in place to do anything with the e-mails.

'I could rant on for ages about all the Web sites that I've sent feedback pointing out errors or deficiencies and received no response, and the error has not been corrected. Worse are the sites that have no way at all of telling them about problems. For example www.peoplesound.com is currently being heavily promoted. But there are broken links on the site, and for a music site to have no way of searching by song title seems mad to me. Yet there is no email address to give them feedback. For me, the cost of doing this needs to be part of the basic business model. Even an auto-responder is something.'

WEB WONDERS

If e-mail provides the basic customer dialogue backbone through the Internet, the Web enables you to broadcast, while giving the customer much more chance to respond than is normally the case with a broadcast medium. This isn't the place to go into what makes a good Web site, but from the point of view of customer communication, the Web site is an important extension to e-mail. (See page 213 for details of *The Invisible Customer*, a book oriented to giving customer service via the Web and call centres.)

Specifically, the Web site can be a repository of information that the customer wants to know. It might be what to do when things go wrong (including, where

66If e-mail provides the basic customer dialogue backbone through the Internet, the Web enables you to broadcast.99

66The Web site can be a repository of information that the customer wants to know.99

possible, actual fixes – for instance the driver software included on PC hardware sites). It might be how to find out more about your products, or just where you are located. Try to list the top 20 queries a customer might have about your company and products – then make sure that in two clicks you can get to that information clearly and quickly on your site. And when the customer gets to the appropriate page, make full use of the flexibility of the Web. If the need is to find your offices, include a map. Include links to train timetables for getting to you, or road route maps or even traffic status pages.

The great advantage the Web has over practically every other means of communicating to the customer is the way you can leverage all the other content of the Web to make your site more valuable. It's not worth your while putting traffic reports on your site, just in case a customer wants to drive to your offices – but it's easy enough to put in a link to someone who can provide that information free.

A final Web thought. Try out your site as if you were a customer. Make sure you use an ordinary PC, connecting with a slow telephone connection – don't just try it out on the direct link in the office. Make sure all those beautiful graphics the designer wanted to include won't slow everything to a crawl. And remember the customers who for one reason or another (using a phone to access the Web, blind customers etc.) don't have access to all the flashy graphics and are dependent on text alone. The Web can do much more for you than be an online catalogue – it's an opportunity to help out your customers 24 hours a day, seven days a week.

PHONE PHREAKS

Although Internet-based communications are increasingly popular, the phone remains a key link between you and your customers. How you handle that connection will influence the customer's relationship. It all starts as they decide

66A final Web thought. Try out your site as if you were a customer. 99

66Although Internet-based communications are increasingly popular, the phone remains a key link between you and your customers. 99

HORROR STORY

NUMBER, WHAT NUMBER?

As this customer found out, it's not enough to make sure that your number is easily accessible. Some companies seem to go out of their way to ensure that there are so many numbers for different requirements that the customer is lost in maze of technical incompetence.

'BT, the UK's main telecommunications provider and now a worldwide corporation, has a scheme where customers can nominate a set of numbers as "key numbers" which receive a discount on each call. When I got my business bill, I found that these key numbers, which should have applied to all three of my business numbers, weren't correctly set up.

'The telephone bill shows four numbers to call for help, for bill enquiries, sales, fault reporting and customer service respectively. I tried the customer service number. After pressing a few buttons on a voice system I spoke to a real person, who said I should ring the key numbers hotline. The hotline said that they could enter new numbers, but to link my lines I needed to call 152, BT's generic business service number. The agent on 152 gave me yet another free phone number to ring. I was rather baffled when the message stated, "Welcome to Orange" [one of BT's competitor telephone companies].

'I went back to 152. Now came the most hilarious bit. I pointed out that the number they had given me put me through to Orange. The agent said "Yes, it's strange, I think it's done that for me too." "What, to put in my BT key numbers I need to speak to Orange?" "Just a minute, I'll check." She came back and told me I needed to speak to the key numbers hotline. "But they were the ones who put me on to 152." She was so sure that she put me through directly to the hotline. When I'd explained my situation, they told me that I would need to speak to sales. Finally, I found someone who could help, only to tell me that the call in which I'd changed all my key numbers a week before had been ignored. Finally, to add insult to injury, they had to ask my address to send me a confirmation letter.

'It's not the cost of the calls – they were all toll-free numbers – but the time taken. Each time I had to dial a different number. Each time I had to give my name, my business name and my phone number. It took a total of seven calls to get a simple transaction made. It's not good enough.'

to call you. How easy is it to find the number? Is it blazoned all over your products and your written communications with the customer? Do you have prominent advertising in the Yellow Pages and an easy to find entry in the White Pages? There's no point in providing phone access if no one can get to the number.

Then there's the number the customers dial. Is it a toll-free number, or do they have to pay? Arguably, toll-free numbers are one of those 'negative when absent factors'. If you are the only company with a toll-free number, it probably won't win you lots of customers. If, however, the norm in your business is to have toll-free numbers and you are the only one without, you will suffer. An increasingly common compromise is the 'lo-call' number where the telephone company gives the customer a local connection charge anywhere in the country.

So, finally, the phone begins to ring. Here's another critical point for your customer service. If the number is engaged or the phone rings for too long, you have already got yourself into the customer's bad books. But worse is still to come. Because chances are, when the phone stops ringing they will hear an interactive voice response system, those keypad-based menu selection devices that are the bane of every customer's life. Such is the distaste that most people have for these systems, they are rapidly replacing programming the VCR as the butt of comedians' jokes.

It doesn't matter how often you tell the customer that an automated voice system is 'for your convenience', they won't be convinced. They know that it is there to save your company money, so there is little point in trying to fool them. This view is shared by Jim Spowart, the Chief Executive of UK insurer and telephone bank, Standard Life. Standard Life handles some 3,000 calls per day in two call centres, but the company has intentionally avoided interactive voice response. Spowart thinks that a customer should always be put straight through to an operator. It works. When you ring Standard Life, you feel relieved.

❝If the norm in your business is to have toll-free numbers and you are the only one without, you will suffer.❞

It's not that interactive systems are totally worthless. Like the banks' automated teller machines, they are a great complement to human interaction. If you want to ring up your bank and transfer cash from one account to another at 3 am, it may be that you would like to do so by simply pushing a few buttons on your phone. But the customer should have the choice.

One intermediate solution that is becoming more possible is natural language voice systems. Here, rather than pressing keys on the phone keypad, the customer talks to the system, which interprets his or her remarks. The technology to support this approach has advanced dramatically in the last few years and is getting more and more practical. Natural language systems have the advantage of not requiring a touch-tone phone – not a trivial point as there are still millions of phones worldwide relying on the old pulse dialling. But more important still, they allow a much richer interface. Instead of asking the customer to choose from a tedious menu, they can say what they want. Even so, such systems are inevitably much more limited than a human being, and again it is worth providing a mechanism for getting direct access to a human being.

When the customer speaks to someone, the aim should be to make this as much as possible a conversation between people who know each other. Contact management systems and customer relationship management systems can help, but the benefits will be maximized if the customer has a mechanism for getting in touch with someone they know, rather than speaking to the first person available in a call centre.

If a customer has to be called back, even more so than with an e-mail, the customer expects a quick response. Generally calling back the same day should be the standard, only shifting to the next day if the call comes very late. The all-too-frequent possibility of no call-back at all should not be an option. Leaving

❝The customer should have the choice.❞

a customer waiting hours or days for a call-back almost denies the existence of the customer. If they were standing in front of your staff it is highly unlikely they would be rude enough to ignore the customer for hours or days on end. The telephone shouldn't be seen as a screen that enables them to do this, but rather an open channel of communication.

(We can only skim the surface of customer service over the phone here – see details of *The Invisible Customer* on page 213 for more information.)

OPENING CHANNELS

When communication with the customer is supported and enhanced it has an inevitable effect on the image of the company. A company that really listens, and really communicates inevitably has charisma. Most of the focus on this chapter has been on making the communication happen. However it is worth giving some consideration to the quality of that communication.

What is the difference between the sort of communication we might get in the hypothetical village store and in your business? The store conversation is, of course, more relaxed. Unless there are other customers, the shopkeeper is not in any hurry. Even then, a good village shopkeeper seems capable of exuding calm and lack of pressure. Then, the village shopkeeper knows you. As we saw in a previous chapter, the more the customer contact staff really know the customer, the better the service. From a communication viewpoint it opens up whole topics of conversation that wouldn't otherwise be available.

That word 'conversation' is an important one. All too often, when you deal with the front line staff of a large company you have a transaction. When you deal with a village shopkeeper you have a conversation. Yes, there are the words

> ❝If a customer has to be called back, even more so than with an e-mail, the customer expects a quick response.❞

> ❝When communication with the customer is supported and enhanced it has an inevitable effect on the image of the company.❞

necessary to undertake the business in hand, but there will also be comments on the weather, village gossip, holidays and family. The business takes place in the context of a human interaction, not a mechanical one.

At a basic level, anyone can have a conversation, rather than just providing a transaction. Comments on the weather or the news can be used with anyone. Where, however, the customer contact staff know and are known by the customer so much more is possible.

Your communication will be as good as your people, and the goals you have set them. If good communication doesn't feature in those goals, don't be too surprised if it doesn't happen. It takes time, it takes effort – but it's worth it for all concerned.

66 Where the customer contact staff know and are known by the customer so much more is possible. 99

66 Your communication will be as good as your people, and the goals you have set them. 99

12

THE TWELFTH COMPONENT

The twelfth component has a mysterious quality. It isn't a general property that can be applied to any business. It is the unique speciality of your company. The aspects of the company that make it different from all its competitors. Every company has something. Many have several unique facets. But how much you develop that difference, and what you make of it, is up to you.

DOES IT EXIST?

The twelfth component is something of a mystery, so much so that to begin with I wasn't even sure that it existed. But the more I have explored it, the more certain I am that there *is* something here, something very special. The emphasis of the twelfth component is uniqueness. It concerns the aspect of your company that is special – so special that it differentiates you from most or all of your competitors. It doesn't have to be big. It doesn't even have to be something generally regarded as positive. But it gives you a unique selling point.

An example: I run a small company called Creativity Unleashed Limited. We provide three services or products (I'm never quite sure which) – writing business books like this, providing business and IT journalism, and offering business creativity training. These subjects are based on the expertise of our prime operational resource – me. In each subject, there is an opportunity to be a little special. There are plenty of people providing business creativity training and consultancy, but not so many who have written a range of books on the subject. There are lots of business and IT journalists – but not so many who have been senior managers in large companies. There are plenty of business authors, but few who can combine practical business experience, the connectedness of being a journalist and the innovation of the creativity practitioner.

I don't claim that any of these advantages are world shattering, but they do combine to give an edge. They make me a little bit special in my fields of operation. And being a bit special to your customers is a critical component of charisma.

That's fine for a one-man band, where the mix of capabilities and experience of an individual is crucial to success, but how about a bigger company? I'd like to suggest that size doesn't make the slightest difference. The special interests and abilities and experience of your people, the special opportunities you have from location to looks – however big your company, using these assets and opportunities wisely will engage the twelfth component.

This is a concept that is very familiar to the marketing fraternity. They call it a USP (unique selling proposition). The key facts about your business, your products, your services that allow you to distinguish it from the opposition in your advertising and all your communications with customers. The twelfth component applies USP to customer service.

USP?

It's worth spending a little time on the subject of USPs, because the concept has been well explored in marketing circles and directly links to the twelfth component, even though it might not always work quite the same way. Ideally

66Being a bit special to your customers is a critical component of charisma.99

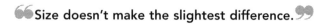

66Size doesn't make the slightest difference.99

a USP should be one that hasn't been grabbed by a competitor. It should be clear, easily understood by any customer. It should be short and sweet enough to incorporate in all your advertising, packaging, letterheads – however you communicate with the world, you ought to be reminding them of that USP.

USPs can be quite sophisticated – the Body Shop's might be something like 'the beauty product shop that cares about the environment'. Or they can be very down-to-earth. 'Number 2, so we try harder' or 'Never knowingly undersold'. Once you have identified that USP it has to be branded on the public's mind as associated with your company. This means repeating it ad nauseam – but it can also mean expanding on it.

A good example would be recent advertising by German car manufacturer BMW. Their USP concerns the quality of their design and manufacture. Rather than just stating this, BMW advertising repeatedly examines the amazing depths their designers go to, to make sure that the product is just right. Sometimes it isn't enough to state your USP – sometimes you have to help people to understand just what it means.

USPs can be compound, combining different advantages your company has, but such mixed messages rapidly become confusing. By the time you've assessed 'we're the pizza company that delivers on time or gives you twice your money back, and it will always be hot or we'll give you another pizza, and if we get your order wrong you'll get a free holiday voucher. Oh, and our drivers can handle cash (yes, they really have change) and credit cards', it has all become rather messy. These might all be unique differentiators from the competition but you've lost the clarity of message that will get through to the customers every time. It would have been better to have made it 'we deliver satisfaction – no excuses' only that's a bit vague, lacking the clear, simple checks that at good USP has at its heart.

> 66 However you communicate with the world, you ought to be reminding them of that USP. 99

> 66 Sometimes it isn't enough to state your USP – sometimes you have to help people to understand just what it means. 99

This single focus and simplicity of a USP is why I say that it is part of, but not all of the twelfth component. The twelfth component is made up of all your unique advantages, not just the prime one you want to beat into the customers' memories. There is a lot more to it.

YOUR ASSETS

From your USP, the search for the whole of the twelfth component extends to your assets as a whole. What do you, as a company, have to offer the customer? Your people, your premises, your equipment, your style and service. Each of these can contribute to your uniqueness.

Each of your members of staff is a person, not just another cog in the machine. This isn't a bit of social worker speak, but a practical assessment of their potential value to the company. There is more to them than the normal requirements of the job will expose. They might be singers or actors, writers or gymnasts. They might be experts on the characters of a soap opera or gardening enthusiasts. Making best use of your people implies being aware of this. You might not have a direct and immediate use for it, but playing to the staff's individual strengths and allowing the customers access to these strengths can provide real advantage.

The same goes for your premises and equipment. So often companies trample all over the unique features of a location to reach standardization. In doing so they are wasting a part of the twelfth component. Visit a town with shops that haven't been just built out of pre-stressed concrete, but have been incorporated into an existing façade. Take a step back and really look, taking in the upper floors as well as the shop front. Often you will see beautiful, unique structures that have been made entirely bland by a standard shop interior that could be in a shopping mall built yesterday rather than a historic building.

Now compare this with the experience of shopping in Liberty's amazing store in London's Regent Street. Quite simply the most elegant department

❝What do you, as a company, have to offer the customer?❞

store in the world, Liberty doesn't try to be another Macy's or Harrods. It doesn't stock everything, but the things it does stock, from its unique fabrics to gifts, carry its special stamp. However, the significance here is that Liberty isn't a faceless box like many department stores. It's a delightful fantasy of a building, inside and out. The unique structure of the Liberty store is made a feature, rather than considered a liability to be walled off and hidden.

Few businesses have the equivalent of a Liberty building to play with, but equally, few make good use of the unique space and structure that every building has to offer. They hide huge portions away in parts never reached by the customer. They hide rather than bring out the uniqueness of the structure. They don't let the building sell for them. This isn't just a consideration for shops, but any building that customers might visit.

The same approach can be taken with every asset your business has access to. You won't bother with all of them, but there are plenty to think about. There are also opportunities to go beyond your current assets, actively to take on new assets with the aim of boosting the twelfth component and your uniqueness.

YOUR OPPORTUNITIES

You aren't limited to the uniqueness that already exists in your asset base. You can recruit, buy, design and build with uniqueness in mind.

Let's start with people. Silly extreme – labour laws permitting, you could employ only front line staff with red hair. It's something special about you. It doesn't mean that you give any better service, but it makes your outlets stand out. Similarly, you might employee people who were stunningly attractive to the opposite sex. Either of these might be a starting point to this component of charisma. It would be better, however, if the unique quality you recruit for in your customer contact staff was something more directly connected to good service. Perhaps that all your staff spoke at least one foreign language, or could sign. Or all your staff had worked for at least two of your competitors and knew what they had to better. Or whatever you choose – you can certainly recruit for distinction.

SIGNED UP TO SERVICE

Finance company Abbey National recently gave an award to a staff member, Gill Dixon. She went out of her way to find a supplier to produce documents for her company in Braille. She then, in her own time, took lessons in signing so that she could give a better service to deaf customers. Other companies might have squashed Ms Dixon's efforts, pointing out that they had a 'company-wide strategy for dealing with disability in customers'. In this case, the staff member's unique drive to communicate with blind and deaf customers was allowed to shine through.

It's even easier with premises. As the Hard Rock Café proved back in 1971, and all its imitators have since, you can influence customers with a unique environment that adds fascination to the main sales experience. They might technically be there to buy a hamburger, but they also get the ambience, a rock museum and the chance to buy plenty of souvenirs. The trouble with this kind of imported uniqueness, as opposed to working with the unique qualities of your building, is that it's too easy to have me-too competition.

You can see that in the competitors of Hard Rock. You can see it even more so in pubs in the UK – so many of them now have a host of random 'antique' items all over the walls that it doesn't constitute anything special. Yet go in a pub where a special effort has been made – where perhaps there is a wonderful collection of clocks, or a real Victorian environment – and it still makes a difference. The essential seems to be to make your unique feature distinctive rather than generic, and to go for it 110 per cent.

66The essential seems to be to make your unique feature distinctive rather than generic, and to go for it 110 per cent.99

How far you go with the uniqueness of your assets depends on budget and inclination, but practically every business can contribute to this feel. I am not going to work through every possible asset, but let's take one common feature of a retail environment – the till. Tills are a wonderful example of an opportunity to be different that is wasted time after time. Let's give them a little thought.

Being at the till is not generally a happy experience. You have made your decision. You want to get your purchase home to enjoy it, consume it or make whatever use of it that you desire. The last thing you want to do is stand in line, then go through a rigmarole with payment and receipts. That's the appeal of Safeway's Shop and Go system (see page 57) – it minimizes the impact of the till. But if we are being creative, it might be that rather than dispose of the till we want to make the experience more pleasurable.

One approach is to look backwards. Many years ago (although I can still remember them in some stores), it was common for cash operations to take place away from the till. The sales assistant would place a receipt and the cash in a cylinder, which winged its way through a pneumatic system to a central cash office. Any change came back through the same tubeway. There was something magical about these antiquated devices. If you could overcome the delay, and make the machinery as transparent as possible it would bring back some of the glamour of shopping. Perhaps the tubes could just be used to collect cash and till receipts, so the customer didn't have to wait for anything to come back, but could have the small-but-satisfying thrill of seeing the cylinder shoot off through the system.

Alternatively you could look sideways. Tills in fast food restaurants are all neatly pre-programmed to handle purchases at a button push per product. They are also very dull. Perhaps they could have some video game technology included, so your purchases mounted up on a screen – animated hamburgers, fries and shakes dancing across the screen so you could always be sure just what you had ordered. Or link the till to arcade machine technology, so you could see your change being pushed out from a huge pile of coins – or even better give the option to gamble, double or quits on your change.

These were just two suggestions. There are many, many more ways to make the till more of a unique attraction (e-mail me at brian@cul.co.uk if you want to look into further options). The point is that even such a mundane, boring item on your asset list can be made into something that gets customers talking about you. This same approach can be taken with any asset that a customer has contact with. The opportunity is there. With appropriate creativity, you can grab hold of it.

FINDING NUMBER 12

It's no coincidence that in addressing the twelfth component we have returned to creativity. The driving force behind so many of the charisma components, creativity is essential for any company that really wants to be in the vanguard of companies with charisma. See page 212 for details of books on enhancing creativity – it's a process that goes hand-in-glove with building charisma.

Coming up with your unique features is an exercise in observation and creativity. What have you got that makes you different, outstanding? What is it about your people, your products, your brands, your environment, and your equipment that makes you unique? But don't stop at that, particularly if your

66 The opportunity is there. With appropriate creativity you can grab hold of it. 99

66 Coming up with your unique feature is an exercise in observation and creativity. 99

current distinguishing features lack strength. Nearly any aspect of your business can become a talking point. Look for areas of customer dissatisfaction, such as the till. To do this, walk through the customer interaction with your company. What do customers experience? What elements of that experience take up a lot of time, or are particularly significant or difficult? Now use your creativity to change them in a way that makes you stand out.

Unlike the other components, number 12 not only varies from company to company, it also changes with time. You may have to do more and more in the other components, but the basics will remain valuable. With this twelfth component, the originality of your ideas will become diluted as others copy and steal from you. Every year or two you will need to reinvent your originality. But it will be worth the effort.

66Nearly any aspect of your business can become a talking point.99

CREATING CHARISMA

Charisma, like creativity, has long been regarded as something you either had or didn't have. Both assertions have proved incorrect. Creativity can be boosted by appropriate techniques. Charisma can be grown with the application of the 12 components. Taking the first steps in capturing customers' hearts follows an assessment of the current position.

WHERE ARE YOU NOW?

As with any change, it is useful to assess the current position before attempting to move forward. This chapter is an encouragement to measure your effectiveness on each of the 12 charisma components, and start moving immediately in areas that will have most impact. It may be that there is uniform failure, or that you exceed expectation in a couple of components but are particularly weak in others. Without a basic assessment of position it is very difficult to be sure of the need. Some components may not apply – not every business can appeal to technical wizardry, for example – but don't assume at this stage that you should ignore any possibility. It's quite possible to imagine technical wizardry in the finance sector, for example.

BASIC ASSESSMENT

In the series of short statements that follow you will be able to assess your status on the 12 components. Don't try to be too quantitative about this. It is enough to rate each measure as high, medium or low on how well you come up to it. If possible, repeat this exercise across a range of staff members from senior management to front line staff. If you have focus groups or other opportunities to interact with your customers, bring them in too.

One very important consideration with the results – don't try to average them out across the different people who have given you input. This way you will smooth out the bumpy parts of the information – but it's the bumpy parts that are most interesting. When someone has identified a component as particularly poor (most of the statements rate low), find out why. Stories are much more important than statistics in great customer service.

1   **Going the extra light year**

  - We don't just go the extra mile, we go the extra light year.
  - Our customers go away with a smile on the face.

> **66As with any change, it is useful to assess the current position before attempting to move forward.99**

- We don't have difficult customers, just interesting challenges.

- We make sure customers get what they *want*, not what our systems are designed to deliver.

- When customers talk about our staff, they say: 'They go out of their way to be helpful.'

- Our staff notice when something needs doing and just do it. They are rewarded for this.

2   If it's broke, fix it

- If in doubt, we believe the customer.

- Our compensation when we get it wrong is more than the customer expects.

- Our compensation is given enthusiastically, not grudgingly.

- We always apologize, even if we don't think it's our fault.

- Compensation is based on the staff member's judgement, not arbitrary rules.

- We demonstrate to our customers that we trust them.

- We demonstrate to our staff that we trust them.

- We provide staff with enough information to be able to act sensibly on their own judgement.

- If a customer tells us we've made a mistake in their favour, we reward them.

- We don't wait for complaints, we fix things proactively.

3   I'm in love with my car

- Our products are unique and quirky.

66Stories are much more important than statistics in great customer service.99

- Our products feature classic design.

- Customers write fan mail to our products.

- Customers form clubs around our products.

- Customers feel affection for our products.

4   They know me

- We give our customers the small company feel.

- We welcome our customers like old friends.

- We write to our customers as individuals.

- Our customer contact staff are great conversationalists.

- We use systems to maximize the information provided to customer contact staff to build a relationship.

- Our staff are genuinely interested in their customers.

- Our staff genuinely like their customers.

5   Star power

- We use the personality of the person at the top of the company to sell the company.

- We constantly ensure that our company's star has media exposure.

- We are prepared to recruit a star to front the organization.

- Our star is always available when needed.

- We make full use of the star quality of our staff members.

6   They're people like us

- We treat our employees as human beings.

- Each customer knows at least one employee by name – their regular point of contact.

- We don't use lapel badges with a name on.

- We do make sure we get to know customers, using our (and their) name.

- We don't use scripts, but have broad guidance.

- We recruit for and encourage staff to be enthusiasts for our products and the interests of our customers.

- We build common ground with our customers.

- If we have a clearly segmented customer base we recruit customer contact staff who will appeal to the different segments of that customer base.

- Our customers trust our staff.

- We allow our staff to be individuals.

7 **Surprise, surprise!**

- We give our customers pleasant surprises.

- We make regular surprise changes to prices and special offers.

- We surprise our customers with unexpected gifts.

- We surprise our lost customers with incentives to bring them back.

- We use creativity techniques to enhance our originality.

- We do things differently from our competitors – so differently that it surprises the customers.

- We have fun, and make dealing with us fun.

8 **Technical wizardry**

- Our products get customers excited.

- We provide customers with products that they didn't know they wanted, but which make them go 'wow!'

- Our products are cool.

- We aim at teens but motivate adults.

- If our main line isn't producing toys for adults we use toys for adults in our selling.

9 They're mine, all mine

- All of our employees are shareholders.

- Many of our customers are shareholders.

- Our regular customers can become shareholders for free.

- We go well beyond the annual report in communicating with customers and shareholders.

- We always include a treat with every communication to shareholders.

- We ask customers what they want us to do.

- When customers make comments we always respond within two days.

- When customer comments require action we always act, or let them know why we're not acting in less than a week.

- We put our customers in control of their interactions with our company.

- We give regular customers extra benefits.

- All our customers regularly meet managers as well as front line staff.

10 Cute and cuddly

- Customers think of our products, staff or company with affection.

- We have a cute mascot that customers identify with.

- Our corporate image is one that our customers relate to naturally.

- We are associated with popular issues and causes.

- Our products demand to be held.

- Our customer contact staff are the sort of people you'd like to be stuck in a lift with.

- We make use of any areas where the company is an underdog to win customer affection.

11 We keep in touch

- We keep up a regular, frequent dialogue with all our customers.

- We listen to what customers say and we act. Every time.

- We tell our customers what is happening throughout every transaction.

- We don't have physical barriers to communication in the customer service areas.

- We don't treat our customers as if they were all criminals to exclude the few who are.

- We use personal e-mails to keep in touch with customers who are online.

- Our Web site gives customers a chance to help themselves.

- We have a single, easy-to-use customer contact number.

- We don't use clumsy interactive voice response systems.

- We have real conversations with our customers.

12 The twelfth component

- Everyone in the company knows what our USP is.

- We make sure all customers and potential customers are well aware of our USP.

- We make use of the special capabilities of each member of staff to extend our uniqueness.

- We make use of the individual nature of our premises to extend our uniqueness.

- We recruit for uniqueness.

- We have built uniqueness into our premises.

- We make our assets feel different and exciting to the customers.

- We think creatively about our everyday assets and procedures to make them unique and exciting for the customer.

RECOGNITION

Before taking any other actions, it is necessary to acknowledge that there is a problem. If you are comfortable with your customer service, there is little need to make major efforts to do something about it. Yet be very careful that you are not confusing comfort and complacency. Your customers' viewpoint may be very different. When I put out a wide-ranging request for case studies and examples for this book, the vast majority were negative. Many of them were bad news stories about companies that pride themselves on their customer service.

The traditional approach to determining perceived customer service quality is to undertake market research. Feel free to do so, but it won't tell you enough. You might discover that 95 per cent of your customers (or at least those who could be bothered to answer a survey) were satisfied. That may still leave thousands dissatisfied. More important, however, we are not looking for satisfaction. If I am hungry, the hunger can be satisfied by eating junk food, but I won't enthuse about it to my friends and relations the way I might after a meal in a great restaurant. Chances are, you are serving up junk service. And that isn't going to give you any competitive advantage.

❝Be very careful that you are not confusing comfort and complacency.❞

FIRST STEPS

Make sure that this awareness of the need is spread throughout the company. Throughout senior management. Through each member of the customer contact staff. Using every medium, every opportunity. Without a proper understanding of the need, there will be no action.

Then consider your responses to the statements you have just read. Look for components that are particularly weak. Reread the chapters on these components, looking for opportunities to change. Exactly what and how will differ so much from company to company that there cannot be a prescriptive answer. This isn't a matter of following a series of well-defined steps, ticking off the boxes as you go. However, it should be possible to identify some areas in need of remedial action.

You may have to change staff. You will almost certainly have to change (and frequently scrap) policies and procedures. You will need to build trust in both your staff and your customers. Even the first steps aren't going to take place overnight. But this is not a cosmetic exercise, it is a transformation.

LONGER TERM

Each component can provide long-term benefit. With the first steps taken you are probably already ahead of the competition. But beware the return of complacency. Your competitors are changing too. New competitors are

66We are not looking for satisfaction.99

66Hunger can be satisfied by eating junk food... Chances are, you are serving up junk service.99

66Beware the return of complacency.99

66New competitors are emerging that lack many of your disadvantages.99

emerging that lack many of your disadvantages. This is a programme for the lifetime of the company, not a six-month blitz.

Over a longer period you will need to revisit your status regularly – perhaps yearly. Different components will become more significant. But overall the need to keep building charisma will go on.

STARTING NOW

There is only one time to make a start on capturing customers' hearts and moving away from junk service. Now.

You should have some action in place within a week of reading this book. Otherwise you have already let down one of the precepts of charisma. You aren't listening and responding. Look at this book as a message from your customers. From everyone's customers. They want change. If you can listen and respond immediately, you will have a huge advantage over the competition. But don't put it off. Fail to act now and you may never get a chance to act at all. Your company is in urgent need of a charisma injection. Now is the time to give it.

66 There is only one time to make a start on capturing customers' hearts and moving away from junk service. Now. 99

66 Fail to act now and you may never get a chance to act at all. 99

FURTHER READING

Where does charisma come from? How do you capture customers' hearts? We have explored 12 components – the books listed here can help expand on some of those elements. They are rarely straightforward books on customer service. Usually there's something different about them. But then, that's the aim of the game.

WOOING THE CUSTOMER

Jay Abraham, *Getting Everything You Can Out Of All You've Got* (Piatkus, 2000)

Abraham is considered one of the greatest marketing gurus in the world, and you can see why when you read this book. Subtitled '21 ways you can out-think, out-perform and out-earn the competition', it's a great guide to enhancing profits. At the centre of the book is the notion that you have to consider the customer a friend. Very brash style, but don't let that put you off.

Paul Dickinson and Neil Svensen, *Beautiful Corporations* (FT/Prentice Hall, 2000)

Itself a monument to style (Svensen is credited as the book's 'designer'), this short book explores the importance of style to the new business. It suggests that one of the key distinguishing factors for the customer is the way a company handles design (with a bit of environmental friendliness thrown in). A trifle pretentious, but still valuable.

David Freemantle, *What Customers Like About You* (Nicholas Brealey, 1998)

A fascinating exploration of the benefit of adding emotional value to the customer relationship. In a book packed with excellent examples, the author of *Superboss* (McGraw-Hill, 1984) shows how much excellence in customer service is dependent not on objective, quantitative matters, but the subjective, touchy-feely world of emotion.

Daniel Goleman, *Emotional Intelligence* (Bantam, 1995)

The classic book on the importance of emotion in the workplace. Goleman concentrates on the effect of emotion on performance and the individual staff member. While not specifically oriented to customer service, this is the starting point of the excursion into the nature of relations, rather than organizational structures, in business.

CREATIVITY

Creativity is fundamental to building charisma. These books give practical assistance in bringing creativity into the corporate culture.

Tony Buzan and Barry Buzan, *The Mind Map Book* (BBC Books, 1993)

A beautifully illustrated guide to the use of mind maps to take notes, structure ideas and aid memory. Written by Tony Buzan, the developer of the mind map concept, with his brother.

Brian Clegg, *Creativity and Innovation for Managers* (Butterworth Heinemann, 1999)

An overview for the busy manager, showing the need for creativity, where it came from as a management discipline, how it is applied, and how to make it work in a company. Puts creativity alongside other business techniques, and provides an agenda for introducing corporate innovation. Very much oriented to providing a corporate culture of creativity rather than specific techniques for generating ideas.

Brian Clegg and Paul Birch, *Imagination Engineering* (FT/Prentice Hall, 2000)

A toolkit for business creativity, providing a practical but enjoyable guide to making creativity work. Introduces a four-stage process for business creativity, equally applicable for a five-minute session or a week concentrating on a single problem. Plenty of depth, but fun too. If you are only going to buy one book on creativity go for this one.

Brian Clegg and Paul Birch, *Instant Creativity* (Kogan Page, 1999)

This book in the *Instants* series provides over 70 different techniques for coming up with new ideas and solving problems, each designed to be used with the minimum of fuss in an instant. Can be used on its own or as a supplement to *Imagination Engineering*.

Brian Clegg and Paul Birch, *DisOrganization* (FT Pitman, 1998)

The middle way is not enough any more: this book applies creativity to the organization, showing how a radical restructuring may be the only answer to coping with the challenge of change.

Roger von Oech, *A Whack on the Side of the Head* (Warner Books, 1983)

Von Oech's laid-back Californian style attacks the blockers to creativity in an enjoyable way. Sometimes feels more like humour than a management text, but none the worse for this, and there is a serious message under the gloss.

Tom Peters, *The Circle of Innovation* (Hodder & Stoughton, 1998)

Peters brings his usual bravado to the subject of creativity. Based on the slides from a series of talks, this book shows Peters complete return to form – he is at his best, hectoring the reader on the crucial necessity of innovation. As the man says, you can't shrink your way to greatness.

Tom Peters and Nancy Austin, *A Passion for Excellence* (HarperCollins, 1994)

Tom Peters and Robert Waterman, *In Search of Excellence* (HarperCollins, 1995)

SPECIALIST CUSTOMER CARE

Alex Birch, Philipp Gerbert and Dirk Schneider, *The Age of E-tail* (Capstone Publishing, 2000)

This fascinating guide to the implications of the Internet for retail business pulls no punches in describing the dangers for existing businesses that don't take the Internet very seriously. While not specifically focussed on customer service, the subject comes in all along the way in how e-tail customers are handled.

Brian Clegg, *The Invisible Customer* (Kogan Page, 2000)

A special case of customer care is dealing with the increasing range of customers we never see, the customers who deal with our companies through call centres and over the Internet. These invisible customers still have the same needs for excellent customer service, but the opportunities and dangers are very specific to the medium. This new book highlights the route to caring for the invisible customer.

Michael Cusack, *Online Customer Care* (ASQ Quality Press, 1998)

An in-depth study of the processes of the call centre (despite the 'online' title it's mostly about telephones). Driven much more by processes and systems than the actual customer service, but a very helpful context provider.

TRUST

Ricardo Semler, *Maverick!* (Arrow, 1994)

Semler's book refines the meaning of trust within a company. It's not a textbook, but the biography of a company. Despite being located in Brazil during runaway inflation and with potentially difficult unions, Semler took a disgruntled workforce and totally changed its motivation by making the workplace a place people wanted to be. Such is the trust that many staff now set their own salaries. This is an amazing example of theory being put into action – and working.

INDEX